♣ ♣

ITALIAN SYSTEM

OF

WINNING BRIDGE

BY

EDGAR KAPLAN

Edited by A. MOYSE, JR.
and ALBERT H. MOREHEAD

A SIGNET KEY BOOK
Published by THE NEW AMERICAN LIBRARY

Contents

Introduction

Edgar Kaplan is the brightest light that has shone for many years in an American bridge world that long seemed destined to be dominated by relatively old men who entered the field twenty to thirty or more years ago. A young man just out of his G.I.'s uniform, Edgar entered the tournament lists in 1947; by 1952 he was among the fifty top American players; in 1957 he had the biggest winning year of any tournament player in American bridge history—a record that still stands—and incidentally won the life masters' individual championship.

But not every champion player is also a competent theorist and writer on the game. Edgar Kaplan is. His analytical articles in the *Bridge World* magazine have won him worldwide respect. He is a teacher of bridge at the successful Card School in New York City. He is co-author of the Kaplan-Sheinwold system of bidding, one of the new and admirable approaches to that difficult subject. And—more pertinent to this book— he is the player that the official United States teams competing for the world championship in 1958 and 1959 called upon to guide them in defense against the bidding systems used by the Italian world champions.

Therefore no person is or could be better qualified to describe the Italian bidding systems, which have earned the respect of every bridge player.

It is true that Italy has won the championship each year, but in 1959 the American pair of Leonard Harmon and Ivar Stakgold, who are players of the Kaplan-Sheinwold System and regular members of Edgar Kaplan's teams, played throughout the match on even terms with Avarelli and Belladonna, the foremost Italian pair, at a time when Avarelli and Belladonna were at the top of their game.

As editors of this book, we have been greatly impressed by the completeness, organization, good writing, clarity and interest that Edgar Kaplan has put into his presentation of the bidding systems the Italians use. Whether you, the reader, wish to use one of these systems or simply defend yourself against opponents who use it, we believe you will find in this book the answer to every essential question. It has been a valued and rewarding privilege to serve as editors of such a fine manuscript and we do not hesitate to recommend it unreservedly.

A. MOYSE, JR.

ALBERT MOREHEAD

Author's Foreword

For the third consecutive year Italy's great bridge team has won the world championship. Three times running the Italians have finished on top of the grueling round robin for the European championship—this alone a striking achievement—and then have routed the finest teams that the United States could field. It is no wonder that America's bridge-playing public, accustomed since the inception of the game to American supremacy in bridge, is asking "Why?"

Why, indeed? Authorities on both sides of the Atlantic are agreed that Italy's team has had no technical superiority over the Americans—if anything, our top stars make fewer errors in play and defense. But the Italians bid better. They have been more accurate in game and slam bidding; they have had many fewer disasters due to partnership misunderstanding. And this has more than compensated for any slim American advantage in play of the cards, for bridge is primarily a bidder's game.

A great deal of the credit must go to the superb *discipline* of the Italian partnerships. American experts rarely play as fixed pairs; they have many different partners, and trust to on-the-spot judgment and to generalized agreements on bidding style to cope with problems as they arise. In contrast, the Italians really work at partnership. They play constantly as pairs and practice frequently together. In consequence, an Italian pair is seldom confronted with a bidding situation it has not met before or discussed exhaustively.

But it is the two modern, scientific Italian bidding systems—the "Neapolitan Club" and the "Roman Club"—that have attracted the attention of every bridge player in the world, in the wake of the smashing victories. These systems have provided the solid foundation for the wonderful partnerships of the world champions. They are complicated and artificial by American standards, but they produce a degree of accuracy beyond the reach of ordinary American bidding. There is an exact meaning for every bid; there is an exact bid for every hand pattern and strength; and many special bidding situations are covered by specific bids. It is not surprising that the sure-footed Italians have the security of knowing what they are doing while their opponents are often merely guessing.

The two Italian systems are quite dissimilar. They share a few modern European bidding trends—"manufactured" reverses that show strength, not distribution; the "canapé" style of bidding shorter suits before longer. But in essence they differ from each other as much as they do from standard bidding methods. Basically, all they have in common is their objective—that pitiless precision which has ground the American teams like wheat between the millstones of the "Neapolitan Club" at one table and the "Roman Club" at the other.

Both systems achieve their accuracy by limiting the opening bid. In the Neapolitan Club, all hands with 17 or more high-card points are opened one club. Thus a one-diamond, one-heart or one-spade opening starts with a much narrower range; opener's rebid can better pinpoint his exact strength and distribution because of this head start. And strong hands can be bid in leisurely comfort, for the one-club opener has no need to jump in order to show strength.

In the Roman Club, one-diamond, one-heart and one-spade openings are limited in distribution rather than in strength. Balanced minimum hands of 11 to 16 points—perhaps one-third of all opening bids—are opened one club, and stronger balanced hands are opened one notrump. The specialized openings at the two level account for many other hand patterns. Thus the remaining distributions, which are opened one diamond, one heart, or one spade, can be described with remarkable accuracy by opener's second bid.

If all this sounds rather simple to you, you are going to be disappointed. Both systems bristle with difficulties—involved, artificial responses to cope with artificial openings and specialized bids that do not mean at all what they seem. To play either system, you must be willing to do a lot of studying and some memorizing. You must find a partner who is willing also. And then you must practice together diligently; you must work at your partnership like the Italians.

For this reason, it is doubtful that either the Neapolitan Club or Roman Club will find universal acceptance here. But although *you* may not care to expend the effort necessary to play these systems, your neighbor may. So any wise bridge player should take the trouble to learn to play *against* these systems. Reading this book will give you a good idea of what you are up against; and the sections on defense may prove to be very useful indeed.

For three straight World Championships mean that the Italian systems are here to stay.

EDGAR KAPLAN

New York, 1959

THE NEAPOLITAN CLUB

This system was devised by Eugenio Chiaradia, Italy's great player and theoretician, in concert with Carl' Alberto Perroux, the non-playing captain of the world championship team. Two of the three championship pairs use the Neapolitan Club:

Pietro Forquet — Guglielmo Siniscalco
Eugenio Chiaradia — Massimo D'Alelio

The Neapolitan Club is, in reality, three systems in one. There are three entirely separate bidding complexes, each with its own framework of opening bids, responses, and rebids, and each with its own conventions and inferences. Which "subsystem" comes into play is determined by the opening bid.

1. The opening bid of one club is an artificial bid used for all hands rich in high cards, regardless of distribution.
2. Opening bids of one diamond, one heart, and one spade are natural bids, promising length in the suit, but limited in strength.
3. Opening bids of one notrump and two clubs indicate hands with a real club suit, but too weak to be opened one club. Due to the level at which they start, auctions following these openings are treated differently from those inaugurated by one-diamond, one-heart and one-spade bids.

The 4-3-2-1 point count is used in valuing hands. Italians call this the "MW" count, for Milton Work, American bridge authority in the days of Auction Bridge, who advocated its use for notrump bidding. *The number of points required for bids as stated in this book refers to high-card points only;* no points are counted for distributional values such as singletons.

I. The One-Club Opening Bid

The one-club bid is the cornerstone of the system. Its presence is felt in every auction, whether or not it is used—the fact that a hand is *not* opened one club is just as revealing and useful as if it were. Therefore, any hand that qualifies for an opening bid of one club *must* be so opened.

The dividing line between one club and all other openings is 17 points in high cards (distribution is not counted). A hand with 17 or more points in high cards is opened one club, a hand with fewer points is not. There is no upper limit —the one-club opening is forcing (the only forcing opening in the system) and embraces standard American forcing two-bids and two- or three-notrump opening bids.

These are one-club openings:

♠ A K J x x   ♡ A Q 10 x   ◇ K x   ♣ x x

♠ A x   ♡ A K Q J x x   ◇ K Q J x x   ♣ ——

♠ A Q x   ♡ K J x   ◇ A K Q x   ♣ K J x

♠ K 10 x   ♡ A Q x   ◇ K J x x   ♣ A x x

As you see, high-card strength, not playing strength (or club length), is the key. Powerful distributional hands without the point count for a one-club opening are very well described in the system by *subsequent* strong bids, and partner is never deceived about high-card content.

There are two minor exceptions to the 17-point rule. Hands of exactly 17 points that contain isolated queens and jacks (which therefore do not carry their full weight) should not be opened one club. If the first example above is changed to:

♠ A K x x x   ♡ A K 10 x   ◇ Q x   ♣ J x

it is no longer a one-club bid. Seventeen-point hands are borderline and judgment is required.

In contrast, you may "violate" and open one club with fewer than 17 high-card points when you are unwilling to risk a pass of your opening bid. For example, suppose you are dealt:

♠ A K J 10 x x   ♡ A K 10 x x x   ◇ x   ♣ ——

This hand has only 15 points, but obviously you must reach game at least. One club must be your opening, for it is your only forcing bid. Open any normal American two-bid with one club even if it does not meet the point-count requirement.

RESPONDING TO ONE CLUB

The first response to one club is artificial. It shows *not* suit length nor even general strength, but only the number of high-card controls—specifically aces and kings—held by responder.* They are shown in a step system similar to Blackwood. Responder counts each ace as two controls and each king as one control. He shows his total according to the following table:

RESPONSES TO A ONE-CLUB OPENING BID

One diamond—no controls

One heart **—one control (one king)

One spade—two controls (one ace or two kings)

Two clubs—three controls (an ace and a king or three kings)

One notrump—four controls (two aces, an ace and two kings, four kings)

Two diamonds—five controls (two aces and a king, an ace and three kings)

Two notrump—six controls or more

Remember that the response shows only aces and kings; queens, jacks, and distribution are not valued at this stage. There is one exception; holding one bare ace and no more than a jack on the side, respond one heart (one control) instead of one spade (two controls). For example, with:

$$\spadesuit \, J \, x \, x \qquad \heartsuit \, x \, x \, x \qquad \diamondsuit \, A \, x \, x \, x \qquad \clubsuit \, x \, x \, x$$

bid one heart over partner's one-club opening, not one spade.

Note that one notrump and two clubs are reversed in the stepped series, showing four and three controls respectively, not three and four. This is to avoid having a weak hand as declarer should the eventual declaration be notrump.

Observe also that no artificial value is assigned to bids of two hearts, two spades, three clubs, and three diamonds. These are reserved as natural bids (showing length in the suit mentioned)—a good six-card suit and no controls. With:

$$\spadesuit \, Q \, J \, 10 \, x \, x \, x \qquad \heartsuit \, x \, x \qquad \diamondsuit \, x \, x \qquad \clubsuit \, x \, x \, x$$

respond two spades to partner's one-club opening. With a seventh spade bid three spades, with an eighth bid four spades.

---

* It is not known yet whether opener has a distributional hand (and needs only aces and kings from partner) or has a balanced hand (and needs points of any description). Aces and kings are always valuable, queens and jacks, fillers, can be shown later if desirable.

** Note exception.

It is not mandatory to jump in *any* six-card suit holding no controls. Responder, with a weaker suit, can answer one diamond—no controls—and then bid his suit at his next turn.

WHEN THE OPPONENTS INTERVENE

Opponent's action directly over the one-club opening does not alter responder's obligation to show his controls. However, it may make it considerably less convenient and more dangerous for him to do so, as the stepped responses must be started at a higher level. The higher the opponents bid, the greater is the distortion in the normal series of responses. Thus a new table of responses is, alas, required for each overcall.

If your opponent doubles, he uses up none of your bidding space, and responses are exactly as if he had passed. (You have an additional call available—the redouble—which you use to show a club suit and no controls.) A one-diamond overcall distorts the responses very little: You pass (instead of bidding one diamond) with no controls, and the one-notrump response necessarily must show a diamond stopper along with the four controls. With four controls and no stopper, you bid two clubs just as if you had only three.

An enemy overcall of one heart causes more trouble, for it uses up more of your bidding room. Now you must pass with no controls or with one bare king (no queens or jacks on the side). One spade shows one or two controls. Other responses are normal (but you must have a stopper to bid notrump) except that the two-heart cue-bid is now available to show six or more controls.

Responses over higher intervening bids are presented in the tables following. Note that they have two features in common: You need more to make any response at all; the minimum bid is likely to require some "fillers" along with the controls.

RESPONSES TO ONE CLUB AFTER A ONE-SPADE OVERCALL
Pass—no controls, or one or two controls with fewer than 6 points
One notrump—one or two controls with a spade stopper
Two clubs—one or two controls, at least 6 points, no stopper
Two diamonds—three controls
Two spades—four controls
Two notrump—five or more controls

RESPONSES TO ONE CLUB AFTER A ONE-NOTRUMP OVERCALL
Pass—no control or one bare control
Two clubs—one (not bare) or two controls

Two diamonds—three controls
Two notrump—four controls or more

RESPONSES TO ONE CLUB AFTER A TWO-CLUB OVERCALL
Pass—no, one, or two controls
Two diamonds—three controls
Two notrump—four controls
Three clubs—five or more controls
All other suit bids show a strong suit and no to two controls

RESPONSES TO ONE CLUB AFTER ANY HIGHER BID
Pass—no, one or two controls
Cheapest notrump bid—three controls or two controls and
    9 points
Cheapest cue-bid—four or more controls
All other suit bids show a strong suit and no to two controls

Observe that even after an overcall two hearts, two spades, three clubs and three diamonds are (except when it is the suit of the overcall) still reserved for hands with good six-card suits and no controls that can be shown.

Whenever responder doubles an intervening bid, he is making a penalty double based on trump strength and gives no information at all about his controls. Should opener decide to take the double out, he can demand information about responder's controls by rebidding in *notrump* at the cheapest level possible. Responder answers in clubs to show that he has no controls, diamonds for one, hearts for two, etc. If opener is interested only in controls outside the doubled suit, he cue-bids that suit. Now responder discounts all controls in the suit he has doubled and makes the next higher bid to show no controls outside the suit, the bid above that for one control, and so on up the line, counting notrump as a suit.

THE DEVELOPMENT OF THE AUCTION

What happens after the first club opening and the artificial, control-showing response? Next, of course, the partners must describe their distribution to each other. But before detailing this process, let us consider the implications of the bids that have already been made.

The one-club opening is forcing on both partners up to the level of one notrump. Even if the response has been the negative one diamond or the discouraging one heart, neither opener nor responder may pass the hand out until a contract of one notrump or higher has been reached.

If the response has been one spade, the partnership has at least 23 points (17 is opener's minimum; 6 is responder's minimum for one spade—either two kings or an ace and some fillers). So neither partner may pass out below *two* notrump.

Any higher response—one notrump, two clubs, etc.—forces the partnership to game.

Bearing in mind the level to which the partnership is forced, opener (unless he has the notrump type hand we will treat of later) begins showing his suits. Suppose he holds:

♠ A x   ♡ x   ◇ A K Q 10 x x x   ♣ A K Q

He opens one club; partner responds one diamond. Clearly, opener must not rebid only two diamonds, for the partnership is forced only to one notrump; responder may pass two diamonds. So opener jumps to *three* diamonds. When the one-club bidder's first rebid is a jump in a suit, the partnership is forced to game, just as if he had opened a standard forcing two-bid. Interchange the spades and diamonds:

♠ A K Q 10 x x x   ♡ x   ◇ A x   ♣ A K Q

Now opener *could* rebid one spade over one diamond without risking a pass, since the forced level (one notrump) has not been reached. But he would be wiser to jump to two spades regardless. This is his last chance to force to game—a subsequent jump will merely beg partner to go on. This delayed jump might be made with:

♠ A K Q 10 x x   ♡ x   ◇ A J x   ♣ A K x

You bid one club, partner one diamond; you, one spade, partner, one notrump; you, three spades. A stray queen or so in responder's hand may produce game, but with nothing he can pass. Even a jump in a new suit by opener at his *third* turn is not forcing; he must jump at his *second* turn in order to insist on game.

Most of the time, opener will have less powerful hands and he shows his suits, without jumping, in the normal order: longer suit first; higher-ranking of two equally long suits first. However, it is a good idea to save bidding room when the response has been one diamond or one heart, so a four-card suit that can be bid at the level of one is usually shown ahead of a longer suit that must be bid at the two level. In another measure to economize on bidding space, opener will tend to bid the *lower*-ranking of two four-card suits, making it easy for responder to bid the second suit. With:

♠ A K x x   ♡ K Q 10 x   ◇ A Q x   ♣ x x

you bid one club: partner, one diamond; you, one *heart*. If responder has four spades, he will be able to bid that suit regardless of how weak he is, for it is below the one-notrump
level to which the partnership is forced. But if opener bids
one spade instead, responder may be unable to bid hearts.
With:

♠ A K x x   ♡ K Q x   ◇ A J x x x   ♣ x

you bid one club: partner, one heart; you, one *spade*. Partner must bid again, so opener will get a chance to show his
second suit. But if opener rebid two diamonds instead, responder could conceivably pass, and a good spade contract
might be missed. (Responder should assume that any major
suit that opener bids at the one level is a four-card suit, until
it is rebid. Thus he needs four-card support to raise. But if
opener's first suit is a major bid at the *two* level [one club: one
heart response; two hearts] responder can assume it is a five-
card suit and raise accordingly.)

If the control-showing response has been one spade or
higher, opener must rebid a suit-type hand at the two level,
but this is no handicap as the partnership is now forced to two
notrump or to game. Suits are shown in normal order, but
opener should still elect to bid the lower-ranking of two four-
card suits, giving partner a chance to bid the other. Opener
should avoid making his first suit-bid in a four-card major:

♠ A Q x x   ♡ A K J x   ◇ K J x x   ♣ x

you bid one club; partner responds one spade. You rebid two
diamonds. A two-heart or two-spade rebid would indicate a
five-card suit.

Responder has an easy time for the rest of the auction, since
his artificial response has so precisely limited his hand. His
first rebid should be in his longest suit (except when he has
a minimum and can raise opener's suit). Next, he shows
whether he has more than the bare controls he has promised
—fillers, good distribution. If he has, he starts bidding features of his hand (honors, singleton, etc.). If he has no
undisclosed values, he can sign off by raising opener's suit,
by bidding notrump, or by passing if the forcing level has
been reached. Let us see how the auction develops in a few
sample hands:

OPENER	RESPONDER
♠ A K x x	♠ 10 x x x
♡ A x	♡ K x
◊ Q J 10 x x	◊ x x
♣ K x	♣ 10 x x x x

OPENER	RESPONDER
1 club	1 heart
1 spade	2 spades
Pass	

The one-club opening shows 17 points or more, the one-heart response shows one king (or a bare ace). Opener rebids in spades to save bidding room, and responder raises to show four-card support and little extra strength. Note that responder does not pass (for one notrump has not been reached) or bid clubs before raising (which would indicate additional values). Opener can safely pass two spades since he knows from the first response that he is off at least three fast tricks and responder cannot have the fillers or distribution to bring the rest of the hand home. With those values, responder would have bid a suit before raising or would have *jump* raised with his already limited hand.

OPENER	RESPONDER
♠ Q J 10 x	♠ K x x x
♡ A	♡ K Q J x x
◊ A K Q J x x	◊ x
♣ Q x	♣ J x x

OPENER	RESPONDER
1 club	1 spade
2 diamonds	2 hearts
2 spades	4 spades
Pass	

After the one-spade response, showing two controls and forcing to two notrump, opener and responder bid their suits in natural order. Responder jumps to four spades over two spades with good support and undisclosed values. All of responder's bids have been highly constructive, but opener passes without a problem. He knows from the first response that he must lose two, and probably three, fast tricks. How many standard bidders would launch into Blackwood with these cards and go down at five spades!

OPENER	RESPONDER
♠ x	♠ K 10 x
♡ A Q J x x	♡ x x x
◇ A Q J x	◇ x x
♣ K Q x	♣ A J 10 x x

OPENER	RESPONDER
1 club	2 clubs
2 hearts	3 clubs
3 diamonds	3 spades
4 clubs	4 hearts
Pass	

The two-club response shows three controls and is forcing to game. Opener describes his distribution naturally; responder bids his suit and then shows a feature of his hand. Opener was keenly alive to slam prospects after the first two responses, but settles for game when it develops that partner has the wrong king. Note that responder is not concerned about bidding four hearts with only three trumps; opener has promised five hearts by bidding them as his first suit at the two-level.

OPENER'S NOTRUMP REBIDS

If opener has balanced distribution and scattered honors—a notrump type opening in standard bidding—he will, naturally enough, make his first rebid in notrump instead of in a suit. How many notrump does he bid? That depends on two factors—his point-count and partner's response to one club.

If the response has been the negative one diamond, opener's rebids are similar to standard American openings: three notrump shows 25–27 points; two notrump shows 22–24 points; one notrump shows 17–21 points, the rest of the range.

A one-heart response promises at least 3 points, so opener is more aggressive. Three notrump is now 23–25 points; two notrump is 21–22 points; one notrump is 17–20 points.

Since a one-spade response shows 6 points and is forcing to two notrump, a different situation prevails. Opener *can* rebid one notrump with a balanced hand of any strength, if he wants to hear partner's rebid. If he wishes to *give* information, opener can jump to two notrump (forcing) with 20–21 points, or to three notrump with 22–23 points.

Any higher response is forcing to game, so opener rebids two notrump with any balanced hand and signs off or probes for slam as the auction develops.

RESPONDING AFTER A NOTRUMP REBID

When the control-showing response has been one diamond
or one heart, opener's one-notrump rebid shows 17 to 20 or
21 points. So responder, with a flat hand, passes holding 0 to 5
points, raises to two notrump holding 5 to 7 points, and jumps
to three notrump holding 8 or 9 points. (With a four-card
major suit responder has other options—see below.)

With an unbalanced hand, responder can sign off in a suit
by bidding two diamonds, two hearts, or two spades. He can
invite in a suit by jumping to three clubs, three diamonds, three
hearts, or three spades. These are encouraging, but not forcing,
bids promising a six-card suit headed by a queen (if the response was one diamond) or by the indicated king (if the response was one heart).

Responder can probe for a suit contract by bidding two
clubs. This is a conventional bid similar to "Stayman" and
asks opener to bid a major. Opener answers two diamonds
with a minimum and no four-card major, bids a major if he
has one (with both majors he bids hearts), and answers two
notrump, three clubs, or three diamonds (the last two with at
least five-card suits) to show a maximum and no major.

If responder has found a suit fit, he can raise and invite
game with 6–7 points or jump to game with more. If he has
not found a fit, responder can sign off by bidding two of a
major, two notrump, or three clubs (three clubs by the responder when he has previously bid two clubs is an absolute
sign-off, a club bust). With better hands, he can jump to
three notrump or force with three diamonds,* three hearts or
three spades to show a rebiddable suit and offer opener a choice
of game contracts. All these responses are much like "nonforcing Stayman" as played in the United States.

When opener jumps to *two* notrump over a one-diamond
response, responder raises to game with 3 points or more.
Three diamonds, three hearts and three spades are forcing
bids, promising five-card suits at least. Three clubs is conventional and asks opener to bid his four-card suits starting
with the lower (if opener's only suit is clubs he rebids three
notrump). Opener and responder now bid their suits "up the
line" at the three level to find a trump fit.

---

* In the sequence one club—one diamond, one notrump—two clubs,
two hearts—three diamonds, the three-diamond bid does not guarantee a
diamond suit. It may be a device to permit opener to bid spades if he
has four of each major suit.

The jump to two notrump over one heart initiates much the same sequences, but responder passes if he has only his announced king and no other features.

When the auction starts one club: response one spade, rebid one notrump, the responses are a little different, for responder has shown two controls and has forced the partnership to two notrump at least. Now responder can bid two of a long suit over one notrump without risking a pass. If he does so, all his subsequent *changes* of suit are treated as forcing, but if he merely rebids his suit at the three level opener may pass.

The two-club convention is used much as described earlier, subject to the forcing-to-two-notrump rule.

Suit jumps to the three level are now unnecessary, so they are forcing bids showing maximum values and a long suit headed by two top honors. With the same strength but a weaker suit, responder can bid two clubs first and then force with three diamonds, three hearts, or three spades. However, three clubs after two clubs is still a sign-off.

Responder's weakest rebid is two notrump in this situation:

OPENER	RESPONDER
1 club	1 spade
1 notrump	2 notrump

This shows a flat 6 or 7 points and denies holding a four-card major suit. Opener may pass with a minimum.

When the response to one club has been one notrump or higher and opener rebids two notrump, or when opener jumps to two notrump over one spade, 4-4 suit fits are located by using the three-club convention described earlier (page 22).

Let us see how all this works:

OPENER	RESPONDER
♠ A 10	♠ Q J x x
♡ K Q x x	♡ J x x
◇ K J 10 x	◇ x x
♣ A K x	♣ Q 10 x x

OPENER	RESPONDER
1 club	1 diamond
1 notrump	2 clubs
2 hearts	2 spades
3 notrump	Pass

Opener could have rebid one heart instead of one notrump,

since this would be forcing; but he does not, for fear that partner might have to rebid one notrump, placing the weak hand as declarer. Next we see the two-club convention in action: Responder bids two clubs with some interest in game and a four-card major; opener answers with his major; responder signs off with two spades. But opener has a near-maximum and knows that partner has 5 or 6 points to bid at all. So he ignores the stop signal and jumps to game.

OPENER	RESPONDER
♠ A Q x x	♠ K J x x
♡ K x	♡ A x x x
◇ A K x x	◇ 10 x x
♣ K x x	♣ x x

OPENER	RESPONDER
1 club	2 clubs
2 notrump	3 clubs
3 diamonds	3 hearts
3 spades	4 spades
Pass	

Every club bid in this sequence is artificial. One club, of course, shows strength; two clubs shows three controls; and when opener rebids in notrump, responder uses the three-club convention in search of a suit. Opener dutifully answers in his lower suit, responder bids up the line, opener follows through, and the fit is found.

OPENER	RESPONDER
♠ A Q x	♠ K x
♡ A K x x	♡ x x x
◇ A x	◇ J 10 x x x x
♣ K x x x	♣ x x

OPENER	RESPONDER
1 club	1 heart
1 notrump	2 diamonds
Pass	

Opener shows good judgment in passing even though he is near maximum strength. Responder has signed off, and he cannot have so much as a good six-card suit headed by the king, for then he would have jumped to three diamonds over one notrump; so where is the game?

ON DEFENSE AGAINST THE ONE-CLUB OPENING

If your opponents are using the Neapolitan Club System, their one-club opening is a signal to you that the hand "belongs" to them. Resign yourself to the fact that only once in a blue moon will you be able to make a high contract. Your defensive bidding must be designed to disrupt enemy communications, not to provide a leisurely search for your own top spot. The one-club opening is at once a warning and an opportunity: A warning because opener announces solid high card values, and either he or responder can double you on the basis of them; an opportunity because neither opener nor responder will show a real suit until the second round of bidding, and if you can get the auction up high and fast they will be in the dark about how well their hands fit.

The basic principle is that overcalls must be predicated *not* on high card values (95 per cent of the time the opponents will have more points than your side), but on distributional values. Don't overcall with a 5-3-3-2 pattern no matter how many points you have, unless you have a near-solid suit. As your pattern shifts to 5-4-2-2 or 5-4-3-1, you should be more anxious to overcall even if your suit is only fairly good. And with 5-5-2-1 or 6-4-2-1 or wilder shape, come into the auction with the least shadow of excuse. If your distribution can destroy the defensive value of enough of the enemy's high cards, you can do an effective and inexpensive job of disrupting their communications. But not otherwise.

The second principle is to overcall immediately at as high a level as your distribution, your suit quality, and the vulnerability warrant. If you jump to two spades over the one-club opening, you are not urging partner to try for game with scattered values. *You should not expect to make game against a one-club opening.* Your two-spade overcall says that you feel relatively safe in disrupting the opponents' auction to a greater extent than would a one-spade overcall. Two spades is stronger than one spade, but stronger in distributional playing strength, not necessarily in points.

No one is vulnerable; right-hand opponent opens one club. What should you do with these hands?

♠ A x   ♡ Q J x   ♢ K 10 x x x   ♣ Q x x

Pass! Your distribution is flat, your values are defensive, and your suit is broken, so you cannot compete effectively. You

have 12 points, but opener has a lot more. Don't try to fight
an elephant with a water pistol.

♠ K Q 10 x x   ♡ x   ◇ Q J 10 x   ♣ x x x

Bid one spade. You have many fewer points than in the first
example, but your distribution is promising, your values are
offensive, and your suit is better. In addition, a one spade overcall may interfere with the control-showing response, whereas
a one-diamond overcall hardly bothers the opponents at all.

♠ x x   ♡ x   ◇ A x x x   ♣ Q J 10 x x x

Bid two clubs. This is not a cue-bid, for the one-club opening
did not show a real suit. You promise good enough distribution and a solid enough suit to interfere at the two level. With
a seventh club, you should jump to three clubs.

♠ x x   ♡ K Q J x x x   ◇ Q J x x   ♣ x

Bid two hearts. With an excellent suit and fine distribution,
you can afford to overcall at the two level. Another heart or
another diamond would warrant a three-heart overcall.

When do you double the one-club opening? Seldom, for one
thing. A double is just as dangerous as an overcall (more,
actually, for you have a flatter hand) and has no preëmptive
value—the control-showing response is not impeded at all.
So double only if you have a standard 16-point one-notrump
opening or better, no more than one point less than opener's
minimum of 17 points. You are then almost on equal terms
with opener, and you can fight for the partial. Also, partner
may have the distribution for a high competitive bid.

What should a one-notrump overcall mean over one club?
This is an idle bid, for you would double with any strong
balanced hand. Therefore, the one-notrump overcall is the
"unusual notrump," announcing a freak hand with both minors
(at least 5-5, usually eleven cards in the two suits) and asking
partner to bid clubs or diamonds at as high a level as he dares.

RESPONDING TO PARTNER'S OVERCALL

Actually, you do not "respond" to an overcall at all. Partner,
in overcalling, did not show you values and ask you to bid
on the basis of them; he was merely trying to impede the
opponents. If you now bid a new suit of your own, it is despite,
not in response to, partner's overcall, and so your suit must be
long and compact. (Incidentally, do not attempt psychic suit

responses to partner's overcall, trying to steal the opponent's suit; opener will double you for penalties, and you will have helped, not hindered, him.)

Normally, your only action will be to raise partner's suit if you have a fit, in order to add to the preëmptive effect. Make your raise immediately to the highest level you can afford; do not hold another bid in reserve for later. The more information you let the opponents exchange at a low level, the better prepared will they be to deal with your later bid when it comes.

Let us see a few examples of bidding after partner overcalls. No one vulnerable, left-hand opponent opens one club, partner overcalls one spade; right-hand opponent passes. You hold:

♡ J x x   ♠ x x   ◇ Q 10 x x x x   ♣ K x

Bid two spades. Remember that you are not trying to bid delicately to find your best contract, you are trying to use up the enemy's bidding room. Two spades does this more effectively than two diamonds.

No one vulnerable, left-hand opponent opens one club, partner overcalls one heart, right-hand opponent bids one spade. Your hand is:

♠ K J x x x   ♡ Q x x x   ◇ x x x   ♣ x

Bid three hearts. You are not trying for a game that cannot be there (opener has 17 points or more; responder has one or two controls). You are bidding immediately as high as you can afford to.

No one vulnerable, left-hand opponent opens one club, partner overcalls two clubs, right-hand opponent bids two diamonds. Your hand is:

♠ x x   ♡ x   ◇ Q J x x x x   ♣ K x x x

Bid five clubs! The opponents know they can make a high contract—the two-diamond response shows three controls and is forcing to game—but they probably don't know where. If you let them find their suit and then you take a sacrifice, you offer them a choice of doubling or going on after they have exchanged information. Make them guess in the blind.

This principle of bidding at once to as high a level as you are willing to reach applies equally to the response to partner's double of one club. With no one vulnerable, left-hand opponent opens one club, partner doubles, right-hand opponent bids one heart. You have:

♠ J 10 x x x x   ♡ x x x   ◇ x   ♣ x x x

Bid two spades. This is not a game try, for opener is strong and
responder has a king. You are simply trying to steal a part-
score. Opener may well be unwilling to risk a suit-bid at the
three level after a weakish response, with a strong hand
announced on his left.

BIDDING IN FOURTH POSITION

When the one-club opening is to your left, partner passes,
and the control-showing response is made by your right-hand
opponent, you are in much poorer competitive position. Opener
has a good idea of how high he can safely bid, and he knows
nearly the full defensive potential of his side in case he wants
to double you. What is more, if the response has been one
spade or higher, opener can pass any overcall around to his
partner for *him* to double, as a forcing situation has been
created. Clearly, the risks are greater and the rewards are less,
so caution must be exercised in intervening.

If the control-showing response has been one diamond or
one heart, you may still be able to overcall at the level of one.
There is not much greater danger here than there is in overcalling directly over the one-club opening, for the response
has been weak; but there is less to gain, for you can no longer
interfere with the response. Your distribution should be quite
unbalanced to warrant action. Still, if you have a good, strong
suit and want to tell partner what to lead, take a chance and
bid.

However, if you have to bid at the level of two, be very
careful. You must have a pattern freakish enough to justify a
bid of two directly over one club. And pay particular attention
to the internal solidity of your suit and to the playing strength
of your hand. Ask yourself whether you would be happy to be
doubled, and if the answer is no, stay out of the auction. There
is not enough to be gained by coming in.

A situation that can work to your advantage is created when
responder, in showing his controls, bids a suit in which you
are strong. Now you can double, a safe and easy action, to tell
partner what to lead and to encourage him to bid your suit
preëmptively or for a sacrifice. Thus, in the auctions:

SOUTH	WEST	NORTH	EAST
1 club	Pass	1 heart	Double

and

SOUTH	WEST	NORTH	EAST
1 club	Pass	2 clubs	Double

the doubles are for penalties—in effect, free overcalls provided by the opponents' system. If you overcall in the suit responder has bid instead of doubling (one club, pass, one spade, *two* spades) you are not cue-bidding but making a *jump* overcall.

Different treatment must be given this auction:

SOUTH	WEST	NORTH	EAST
1 club	Pass	1 diamond	Double

After the negative one-diamond response, it is still possible that the hand belongs to your side. So you must have some way to bid a strong balanced hand, and this double is for take-out, equivalent to the immediate double of one club. But if the control-showing response is one heart or higher, pass any balanced hand—even 18 or 19 points. The opponents have at least half the high cards in the deck, and your partner has a complete bust.

In fourth position also, the one-notrump overcall (one club, pass, one heart, one notrump) cannot have a natural meaning, so it is once again the "unusual notrump" announcing a freak hand with both minors. Obviously, this bid should not be used over a constructive response with fewer than eleven cards in clubs and diamonds.

COMPETING LATER IN THE AUCTION

The more information the opponents have been allowed to exchange, the more dangerous and the less useful is any bid that you make. In general, therefore, you bid at your first turn or not at all. But there is one position that calls for later action. This is when you have a three-suited hand and pass over one club. Opener rebids—his first real suit—and now you may double for takeout. For example, suppose you hold:

♠ K 10 x x   ♡ x   ◊ A Q x x   ♣ K J x x

One club is opened at your right. You pass, since none of your suits warrants an overcall. One diamond is the control-showing response. Partner passes. Opener rebids one heart, and here you double, asking partner to bid as high as he can in one of the three unbid suits. If the response is more constructive, or if opener's rebid is at the two level, you need more strength for the delayed takeout double. But the pattern should be unvarying; either 4-4-4-1 or 5-4-4-0, short in opener's real suit.

The only other occasion you should have to step into the

middle of the opponents' auction is to double conventional or
false bids for the lead. The double of the conventional two-
club bid over opener's one-notrump rebid, or of the three-club
bid over his two-notrump rebid, demands a club opening lead.
And in suit auctions, be alert to double responder's second
"real" bid—this is most often a feature-showing bid, not a
suit, and if it appears that partner will have the opening lead
this may be a good time to help him out.

Let us close this section with two examples of defense
against the Neapolitan one-club opening:

South, dealer
North-South vulnerable

```
                        NORTH
                        ♠ x x
                        ♡ x x x
                        ◇ Q 10 x x x
                        ♣ A 10 x

        WEST                            EAST
        ♠ Q 10 x x x                    ♠ J x x
        ♡ Q J 10 9 x x                  ♡ A K x
        ◇ ——                            ◇ J x x
        ♣ x x                           ♣ x x x x

                        SOUTH
                        ♠ A K x
                        ♡ x
                        ◇ A K x x x
                        ♣ K Q J x
```

SOUTH	WEST	NORTH	EAST
1 club	2 hearts	Pass	4 hearts

West jumps to two hearts over one club not to "show" anything to partner, but to prevent North-South from exchanging
information. North cannot show his two controls over a two-
level overcall, and must pass. East, with his only defensive
tricks depreciated by partner's bid, takes a premature sacrifice.
And what can South do but double and collect a measly 100
or 300 points in exchange for his slam? He is pretty sure that
he is being robbed—and North is certain of it—but neither
can start bidding broken suits at the five level. Note that a
one-heart overcall by West and a two-heart response by East
would have little effect. North could show his controls over

one heart, South could bid his suit and would romp into a slam when supported.

South dealer
North-South vulnerable

NORTH
♠ Q 10 x x
♡ K J x
◇ J x
♣ A x x x

WEST
♠ x x x x
♡ x x x x
◇ x
♣ Q x x x

EAST
♠ K x
♡ Q x x
◇ K x x x x x
♣ J x

SOUTH
♠ A J x
♡ A 10 x
◇ A Q 10 9
♣ K 10 x

SOUTH	WEST	NORTH	EAST
1 club	Pass	2 clubs	3 diamonds
Double	Pass	Pass	Pass

Unfortunately, this is an actual hand from the 1958 World Championship matches. The American East's jump overcall of three diamonds is a horrible example of precisely what not to do. After North shows three controls, even a two-diamond bid is unthinkable. East had just the wrong hand to bid with— flat distribution, a very weak suit, and scattered defensive values that might stop a slam. He was held to two tricks— down seven, doubled. The fine Italian defense was helped considerably by the control-showing response—by trick two, South knew where every ace and king was.

II. One-Diamond, One-Heart and One-Spade Opening Bids

In the Neapolitan System, auctions that start with an opening bid of one in a suit other than clubs will seem much more familiar to players accustomed to standard bidding methods. Because a one-diamond, one-heart or one-spade opening is a natural bid, promising length in the bid suit, many hands will be bid identically by a Neapolitan pair and by a standard pair. But there are differences too, particularly with two-suited hands.

In normal bidding styles, a longer suit is generally bid first, a shorter suit next; in Neapolitan bidding, the short suit is more frequently bid first, the longer suit secondarily. In standard systems, opener may, for convenience, bid his short suit first; similarly, in the Neapolitan System opener may, for ease in rebidding, bid his long suit first. But where responder, in normal bidding, tends to take opener back to his first suit except with a marked preference for the second, the Neapolitan responder tends to leave opener in his second suit. This allows opener to bid his second suit at even a fairly high level in a competitive auction, for responder knows that it is playable and he need not show preference and take opener back to the first suit.

Another variation from normal bidding comes in opener's rebid. Rebids that show great power in standard systems—jumps, reverses, etc.—show a good deal less in Neapolitan bidding, for they are limited by opener's failure to start with one club. Strong rebids are predicated primarily on playing tricks, on *suit* strength, not high-card strength. Opener treats as strong any hand of 14 to 16 high-card points that has good distribution and honors concentrated in long suits; he considers any hand with less strength, poor distribution, or scattered honors, as a minimum. These are strong opening bids:

♠ A K Q 10 x	♡ K Q J x	◇ x x x	♣ x
♠ x	♡ A Q 10 x x	◇ A K J x x x	♣ x
♠ A K J	♡ x x	◇ A K J x x x	♣ x x
♠ x x x	♡ A K Q 10 x x	◇ A Q x	♣ x

These are not strong opening bids:

♠ K 10 x x x	♡ K Q x x	◇ A K x	♣ x
♠ A	♡ Q 10 x x x	◇ K J x x x	♣ A

♠ J x x x   ♡ A Q   ◇ K J x x x   ♣ K Q

♠ Q x x   ♡ A K Q 10 x   ◇ K x x   ♣ Q x

In deciding whether or not to open the bidding, you can forget that you are playing the Neapolitan System—if you have a normal, standard opening, you bid here too. However, to decide in which suit to open, you must remember the system and consider two factors:

1. Are you going to make a strong rebid—a jump or a reverse (the bid of a second suit higher-ranking than your first at the level of two or higher)—or a minimum rebid?

2. What is your distribution?

With 4-3-3-3 distribution you have no problem. Open in your four-card suit (unless it is clubs—see page 48) regardless of its quality.

♠ x x x x   ♡ A J x   ◇ A x x   ♣ A x x

Open one spade. Any four-card suit is biddable.

All other one-suited patterns (5-3-3-2, 6-3-3-1, 7-2-2-2, etc.) are of course opened in your long suit unless it is clubs. With a long suit and a "strong" opening, you intend to jump in your suit at your next turn.

With 4-4-3-2 distribution, you open in your higher-ranking suit, intending to rebid in your lower-ranking suit (or in notrump). Never reverse with this distribution; if a hand of this flat shape were strong enough for a reversal, it would have been opened one club.

Treat 4-4-4-1 distribution just as if it were 4-4-3-2. Pick your two best suits and bid them both, starting with the higher-ranking.

♠ Q x x x   ♡ K x   ◇ A K Q x   ♣ Q x x

Open one spade, your higher-ranking suit. Disregard suit quality.

♠ J x x x   ♡ A K x x   ◇ x   ♣ K Q x x

Open one heart. Pick hearts and clubs as the two suits you want to bid, one the basis of their high-card content, and begin with with the higher-ranking. However, if partner responds one spade, you will raise instead of showing clubs.

With 5-4-2-2 or 5-4-3-1 distribution, you should want to open with your four-card suit and rebid in your five-card suit.

But if your five-card suit is the higher-ranking, this would be a reverse; and you may reverse only if you have a "strong" opening bid. Otherwise you must lie about your distribution and open the long suit first.

♠ A K Q x x   ♡ A Q J x   ◇ x x   ♣ x x

Open one heart, intending to bid spades at your next opportunity. This will be a reverse, showing a heart suit, a *longer* spade suit, and a strong opening bid.

♠ A Q J x   ♡ A K Q 10 x   ◇ x x   ♣ x x

Open one spade, intending to *jump* in hearts at your next turn. This will show a spade suit, a long heart suit, and a strong opening bid.

♡ K x x x x   ♠ K J x x   ◇ A J x   ♣ x

Open one spade, and rebid in hearts without jumping. Partner will play you for at least as many hearts as spades and possibly more, but this cannot be helped. You want to bid both suits, and you may not reverse with a minimum opening.

Just as in standard bidding, you may rebid a good five-card suit and conceal a weak four-carder.

♠ A x x   ♡ A Q J x x   ◇ J x x x   ♣ x

Open one heart, intending to rebid two hearts. This is particularly important in Neapolitan bidding, since partner tends to assume that your second suit is the better, and will pass, rather than give a preference, with an indifferent holding in both suits.

Treat 5-4-4-0 distribution as if it were 5-4-2-2, picking your stronger four-card suit to be bid.

With 5-5-2-1 or 5-5-3-0 distribution, open in your higher suit and rebid in the lower-ranking. Jump at your second turn with a strong opening.

When you have 6-4-2-1 or 6-4-3-0 distribution, you would like to open with your four-card suit and jump or reverse in your six-card suit at the two level, but you may do this only if you have a strong opening bid. With a minimum hand, open with your six-card suit and rebid it. (The second suit is not shown until the third round of bidding.)

You can show 6-5-1-1 or 6-5-2-0 distribution very accurately when you have a strong opening bid and your six-card suit is the higher-ranking. Open in the shorter suit and reverse into the longer, just as if the suits were 5-4, then rebid the shorter suit.

However, you may handle all the freak distributions (6-5, 6-6, 7-5, 7-6) like the 5-5 two-suiter, opening the higher-ranking suit and rebidding in the lower—at the cheapest level with a minimum, jumping with a strong opening. (If your second suit is of six cards or longer, you may *double* jump in it if bidding economy permits.) Remember, though, that freak hands with strong compact suits may be opened one club even when the point-count does not warrant it.

The general rules governing two-suiters, then, are these:

1. If you reverse you have a strong opening, and your second suit is longer than your first.
2. If you jump you have a strong opening, and your second suit is of five cards or more, at least as long as your first.
3. If you neither jump nor reverse you have a minimum opening and partner cannot be certain of your distribution. But you are more likely to be longer in your second suit than longer in your first.

The only exception occurs when you have a four-card club suit; you may have a strong 6-4 or 5-4 hand and want to reverse, but you cannot open one club. (When you have five clubs or more there is no problem; as you will see [page 48], you open two clubs.) With a four-card club suit, a five- or six-card side suit, and a strong hand, open in your higher suit and then jump in clubs.

    ♠ x x   ♡ x x   ♢ A K Q 10 x   ♣ A K 10 x

Open one diamond, and rebid three clubs over partner's response. This will not be confused with 5-5 distribution, for then you would have opened two clubs, not one diamond.

RESPONDING TO ONE DIAMOND, ONE HEART, OR ONE SPADE

Responses to these opening bids come very close to standard bidding methods. A suit response at the level of one is unlimited and forcing, but may be made with as little as 5 or 6 points. A new-suit response at the two level is unlimited and forcing, and promises more than minimum values. The one-notrump response is a sign-off. Single raises are weak, jump raises are stronger, but limited. The jump shift is very strong, forcing to game. All this is refreshingly normal, and only a few strictly "Neapolitan" variations will crop up in the detailed presentation that follows.

First, how much do you need to respond at all? Opener's hand is limited by his failure to start with one club, but don't pass him out on that account. Distributional values may provide a game; you may find a better suit (remember, partner may well have a suit longer than the one he opened); and it makes life too easy for the opponents when you pass the opening bid. So the normal 5 to 6 points suffice for a response. However, pass with less.

Bid your suit if you can. At the level of one you should respond in a suit even with the minimum of 5 or 6 points. But if your suit is lower-ranking than opener's and you must go to the two level to bid it, you should normally have at least 10 points for the suit response. A two-over-one response virtually *forces the partnership to the level of two notrump or higher,* so use care. Exceptionally, you may go to the two level with 8 or 9 points if you have a long, strong suit; then you can rebid it at the three level to sign off.

If you cannot bid a suit, respond one notrump. This shows 5 to 9 or 10 points and denies possession of any four-card suit higher-ranking than partner's. If you respond one notrump to a one-heart opening, you may have a club suit or a diamond suit, but you have no more than three spades.

Suppose partner opens one heart. What is the response with these hands?

♠ x x x x   ♡ Q x   ◇ x x x   ♣ A 10 x x

Bid one spade. Do not skip over a suit to respond one notrump. Any four-card suit is biddable; partner will not raise without four trumps.

♠ Q x x   ♡ x x x   ◇ K x x   ♣ A Q x x

Bid two clubs. With 11 points you are willing to get up as high as two notrump, so show your suit.

♠ K x   ♡ x x x   ◇ J x x   ♣ A J 10 x x

Bid one notrump. You are too weak to bid your suit at the two level.

♠ x x   ♡ x x   ◊ A K J 9 x x   ♣ J x x

Bid two diamonds. You have only 9 points but can sign off on the next round by rebidding your diamond suit.

With four cards or more in partner's suit, it is desirable to raise him directly. A single raise is a limited, discouraging response, showing 5 to 9 or at most 10 points and at least four trumps. A *jump* raise is a limited but encouraging response, showing four-card or longer support with a minimum of 9 or 10 points and *no more than 12 points*. This jump is non-forcing—opener will pass with a bare minimum. The *double* jump is semipreëmptive as in standard bidding.

Partner opens one spade. What is the response in these examples?

♠ J x x x   ♡ x x   ◊ K x x x   ♣ Q x x

Bid two spades. Game is most unlikely, as opener's hand is limited, but your raise may shut out the opponents.

♠ A J x x   ♡ x x   ◊ K x x x   ♣ Q x x

Bid three spades. This urges opener to go to game, but does not force him.

♠ Q J x x x   ♡ x x   ◊ A J x x x   ♣ x

Bid four spades, a shutout bid. If you go down, the opponents could probably have made a high contract of their own. (Avoid this double jump when you have as many as three control cards—ace and kings.)

♠ Q J x   ♡ x   ◊ K Q x x x   ♣ x x x x

Bid two spades, an exception. This is bid because you are too weak to respond two diamonds, and one notrump is distasteful with an unbid singleton. However, it is a VIOLATION to raise with only three trumps, so avoid this whenever possible. Remember, partner may have opened on four to the five-spot.

Responder's jump to two notrump over the opening bid is like the jump raise, encouraging but nonforcing. It promises 11 or 12 points, balanced distribution, and stoppers in all unbid suits. With the same distributional requirements and 13 to 15 points, you may jump to three notrump. However, tend to avoid these responses and bid a suit instead if there is anything at all about your hand to make you doubtful about notrump: for example, good support for partner's major suit, a dubious stopper in a side suit, or a lack of tenace combinations that you want led up to—suggesting that notrump may play better with your partner as declarer.

When you have 13 points or more, and thus are sure that you want to go to game, you cannot use the limit jumps described previously. You can always bid your suit and force for one round, but you may be unable to find a forcing rebid. For only your first change of suit is forcing; a subsequent bid in a new suit is encouraging, but may be dropped by opener *unless it is a reverse* (a second suit higher in rank than your first). Responder's reverse is forcing to game, and this is your principal method of bidding strong hands. If necessary, you may have to "invent" your first suit in order to force by reversing into your real suit with your rebid. For example, suppose partner opens one diamond and you hold:

♠ K J x x x x   ♡ x x   ◊ K x   ♣ A Q x

If you respond one spade, you will have no satisfactory second bid (a jump to three spades at your second turn is again a limit bid). So you bid two clubs and reverse into spades over partner's rebid! This forces to game and guarantees a genuine spade suit—the *second* suit is never invented. Opener will probably raise your club "suit" if he has four cards in support —he should not assume that your first suit is false when you reverse, merely that you are longer in your second—but he will avoid committing the partnership to a high club contract if you shy away from the suit. Therefore, in choosing your first suit to prepare a responder's reverse, be as natural as possible—if you have no four-card suit that will do, bid a suit in which you have some high honor.*

If you have 13 points or more, and a four-card or longer fit with opener's major suit, you bid a suit of your own and then "reverse" into partner's suit with a jump to the three-level.

Responder holds:

♠ A Q x x   ♡ K x   ◊ x x x   ♣ A J x x

OPENER	RESPONDER
1 spade	2 clubs
2 diamonds	3 spades

* If you "invent" a heart suit, preparing a reverse into spades, be sure that you have at least three hearts. Opener may get enthusiastic about a major suit—remember, he can have five hearts and open one diamond.

Note that a simple preference to two spades is not enough. This would describe the same strength as an immediate limit jump raise, and it is nonforcing.

THE FOUR-DIAMOND CONVENTION

What does one do with this same responder's hand if opener, by rebidding his suit, prevents him from "reversing" with a *jump* to the three level?

OPENER	RESPONDER
1 spade	2 clubs
2 spades	?

Three spades here would be a limit raise, and even the jump to four spades is insufficient—you may merely be taking a shot at game with three trumps and a fairly good hand. You must bid four diamonds! RESPONDER'S JUMP TO FOUR DIAMONDS IS A CONVENTIONAL BID ANNOUNCING THAT OPENER'S REBID HAS ROBBED HIM OF HIS REVERSE.

Another example of the four-diamond convention is this sequence:

OPENER	RESPONDER
1 spade	2 clubs
2 hearts	4 diamonds

Responder could still have "reversed" with a jump to three spades—how has he been robbed of his reverse? He must have intended to reverse into *hearts;* now he can no longer do so. To use the sequence above, responder might hold:

♠ x x   ♡ A K J x x   ◇ K x   ♣ A 10 x x

A third case in which the four-diamond convention is used is when, after a *one-over-one* response, opener bids two of a lower-ranking suit. Here a preference is a sign-off:

OPENER	RESPONDER
1 heart	1 spade
2 diamonds	2 hearts

So the jump preference to *three* hearts is a limit raise, not a reverse. Responder's reverse into opener's first suit is shown by the conventional four-diamond bid:

OPENER	RESPONDER
1 heart	1 spade
2 clubs	4 diamonds

There is only one other way (besides reversing) that you can show a powerful hand as responder. This is with an immediate jump in a new suit (one heart—two spades, etc.). You should jump-shift rather than reverse when you have at least 14 points with a solid or semi-solid suit (K-Q-J-x-x-x or better) and want to set the trump suit once and for all. However, for the jump shift in clubs (one heart—three clubs, etc.) you cannot afford to be so careful about the solidity of your suit. Obviously you did not have the option of *reversing* into clubs, there being no lower-ranking suit to bid first.

DEVELOPMENT OF THE AUCTION

As we consider in detail the sequences that follow the openings of one spade, heart, and diamond, bear in mind that there are very few forcing situations. Opener has limited his hand by failing to bid one club; responder limits *his* hand if he does not reverse (or jump-shift originally). Either partner may decide at almost any point that the auction has gone far enough. When responder bids a new suit and so is unlimited, he is usually the one who decides to stop at a partial, go to game, or try for slam.

After a one-over-one response, opener makes his rebid— strong or minimum—as originally planned. If responder has bid opener's second suit, opener raises—a single raise with a minimum hand, a jump raise with a strong hand. (Note that any raise of a suit that has not been rebid promises four-card support. If a major is raised, the trump suit is established and further bids in new suits may be "false"—cue-bids for slam or feelers for game.) With a flat hand, opener generally rebids one notrump, but he may, instead, jump to *two* notrump. This shows a good 16 points or the sort of scattered 17 points that is not opened one club.

Responder will pass this jump to two notrump with a balanced hand and 8 points or fewer, raise to three notrump with 9 points or more. Any *new* suit that responder bids over two notrump is a one-round force, probing for the best contract.

CONVENTIONAL THREE-CLUB BID BY RESPONDER

A rebid of responder's first suit is invitational but nonforcing, showing about 8 points and a six-card suit. Should responder wish to *sign off* at three of his suit, he must first bid three clubs. This is conventional, and forces a three-diamond reply; now responder closes the auction by bidding his suit.

For example:

OPENER	RESPONDER
1 heart	1 spade
2 notrump	3 clubs
3 diamonds	3 spades *
Pass	

After a two-over-one response, opener again makes his planned rebid, strong or minimum. However, he should prefer to rebid a five-card major suit rather than show a second suit—opener will get another chance to bid, for the response has forced the partnership to the level of two notrump. The one exception to this forcing principle is in a sequence like:

OPENER	RESPONDER
1 spade	2 clubs
2 diamonds	2 spades

Responder has limited his hand—he could "reverse" by jumping to *three* if he wanted to force to game—so opener may pass with a bare minimum.

If opener rebids two notrump over a two-level response, he describes a *minimum* balanced hand. In the Neapolitan System, you generally show weakness when you go right to the level to which the partnership is forced. If you are stronger, you stay below the forcing level and exchange information. Consequently, this auction, which is strong in standard bidding:

OPENER	RESPONDER
1 spade	2 hearts
3 diamonds	

shows no extra values in Neapolitan style. Opener is simply following through with his minimum rebid and conceivably may be passed right there.

After a one-notrump response, game is unlikely. Opener passes or makes his planned rebid according to his distribution. As in standard bidding, this sort of auction:

OPENER	RESPONDER
1 heart	1 notrump
2 clubs	2 diamonds

is a complete sign-off.

---

* A four-club bid here would show six clubs, four spades, and a weak hand.

After a single raise (one heart—two hearts), opener can invite game by raising to three, or can probe for game by bidding a new suit (forcing, since a trump suit is established). As in standard bidding, responder signs off by returning to the trump suit.

OPENER	RESPONDER
1 spade	2 spades
3 diamonds	3 spades

After a jump raise (one spade—three spades) opener passes with a bare minimum, goes to game with extra values, or tries for slam by bidding a new suit. Likewise, over the limit jump response of two notrump (one diamond—two notrump) opener can pass, bid game, or force with a new suit in search of a trump contract. Any bid in a new suit is forcing. The rebid of his first suit is discouraging.

After a jump shift or responder's reverse, the partnership is forced to game. Until a trump suit has been established, suit bids are "honest"—showing length—but after a fit is found, new suit bids show features for slam or stoppers for notrump. (Remember that jump shifts in diamonds, hearts or spades set the trump suit immediately.) If responder's reverse is made by means of the four-diamond convention, opener signs off by returning to the agreed upon suit. Any other bid is a slam try.

Very few of the sequences described are much affected by an opponent's overcall. Raises are identical. Notrump bids have the same limits (naturally, notrump responses and rebids now promise substantial material in the enemy suit). Free responses in suits are unlimited and forcing, still promising 10 points or more when bid at the two level. Responder's reverses and jump shifts are his strong bids, and an even more powerful action is added—the cue-bid of the opponent's suit. As in standard systems, this is an immediate slam try, showing first-round control of the cued suit. Doubles of overcalls are for penalties.

An opponent's takeout double creates new situations. Over the double, responder redoubles or jumps to two notrump with any hand from 12 to 13 points on up. (Two notrump shows a singleton or void in opener's suit; redouble promises two cards or more.) Any action other than redouble or two notrump limits responder's hand to 12 points at most.

A one-notrump response over the double indicates shortness

in opener's suit and 5 to 8 points. Raises and jump raises are made as if the double had not intervened. New-suit responses show distributional values and are nonforcing regardless of level (responder should *jump* in a good suit with 8 to 12 points). Responder will pass any balanced hand of 0 to 7 points; he may also trap pass with 8 to 12 points, hoping to double some subsequent bid. Any later action, after passing, shows the latter type of hand.

If the takeout double is made by fourth hand, over the response, opener will redouble with four-card support for responder's suit and a strong opening bid; he will raise with four-card support and a minimum opening. With tolerance for responder's suit he may pass. Otherwise he makes his intended rebid.

Third hand, the opening bid may be made a point or two lighter, just as in standard bidding. No response by a passed hand is forcing—jumps are merely encouraging, showing maximum values for a pass. Responder cannot prepare for a reverse by bidding a false suit, since he may be dropped in his bid; but then if responder had enough strength for a reverse he would not be a passed hand. A new suit at the two level may be bid in response a little more freely, for the force to two notrump no longer exists. Responder may still bid even a very weak four-card suit at the *one level;* opener should not pass a one-over-one response except with a completely balanced subminimum hand.

Let us see some examples of the auctions that follow one-diamond, one-heart, and one-spade opening bids:

OPENER	RESPONDER
♠ K Q J x x	♠ x x
♡ x x	♡ Q x x x
◇ A K 10 x	◇ x x
♣ K x	♣ A 10 x x x

OPENER	RESPONDER
1 diamond	1 heart
2 spades	Pass

With a strong hand, opener can afford to bid "normally"—short suit first. Responder is too weak to go to the two level, so he shows the suit that he can bid at the one level. Opener completes the picture of his strength and distribution by reversing with a jump to two spades. (Note that opener does not

bid one spade—a rebid at the one level is never a reverse.
Opener might bid one spade here with a minimum hand that
had five strong diamonds and four weak spades; had he been
unable to show the spade suit at the one level, he would have
concealed it and rebid diamonds.) Responder is happy to pass
two spades; he knows that partner has more spades than
diamonds, and he knows that his hand will not produce game,
for opener—although "strong"—was not strong enough to
open one club.

OPENER	RESPONDER
♠ A K 10 x x	♠ Q x
♡ A K Q x	♡ J 10 x x
◊ x x x	◊ K 10 x x
♣ x	♣ K Q x

OPENER	RESPONDER
1 heart	3 hearts
3 spades	4 hearts
Pass	

Again we see the strong opening bid in the shorter suit preparing a reverse into the longer. Responder employs the
limited jump raise—he is willing to stop at a partial if opener
has no extra values. Opener puts out a mild feeler for slam
by bidding three spades (this shows a spade *control*, not a
spade *suit*, for hearts have been established as trumps). But
responder is not interested; he has close to maximum points,
but poor values for slam.

OPENER	RESPONDER
♠ x x	♠ x x x x
♡ Q x x x	♡ K x x
◊ A K J x x	◊ Q x x
♣ K x	♣ Q J x

OPENER	RESPONDER
1 heart	1 spade
2 diamonds	Pass

Here opener has a minimum, and can afford to bid his short
suit first only because it is higher-ranking. Responder can bid
his anemic suit safely, as opener will not raise without four-
card support. Opener's two-diamond rebid denies a strong
hand, for he has neither reversed nor jumped. Therefore

responder passes. Note that he does not give a preference back to hearts; opener's diamonds are likely to be longer than his hearts.

Exchange opener's hearts with his diamonds, and he still opens one heart, but would rebid two hearts.

OPENER	RESPONDER
♠ x x	♠ A x x
♡ Q 10 x x	♡ A K J x
◇ A K J x	◇ x x x
♣ K x x	♣ A x x

OPENER	RESPONDER
1 heart	2 clubs
2 diamonds	3 hearts
4 hearts	Pass

Holding two four-card suits, opener starts with the higher-ranking. Responder is too strong for the nonforcing jump raise; therefore he lays the groundwork for a reverse by bidding two clubs—he would prefer to have four clubs, but must make do with what he has been dealt. Opener follows through with his minimum rebid (over a one-spade response he would have rebid one notrump instead) and responder jumps to three hearts, completing his forcing-to-game reverse. Opener has no extra values and bids at once to the level to which he is forced, signing off.

OPENER	RESPONDER
♠ J x x x	♠ K x x
♡ Q x	♡ K J x
◇ A K 10 x	◇ Q x x x
♣ K x x	♣ Q 10 x

OPENER	RESPONDER
1 spade	2 notrump
Pass	

Again, opener starts with his higher-ranking four-card suit. (He can bid so weak a suit because responder seldom raises without four trumps.) Responder has a classic jump to two notrump—11 points, even distribution, stoppers, and tenaces. This jump is invitational, not forcing, and opener, with his skinny minimum, declines the invitation.

OPENER	RESPONDER
♠ K x	♠ Q x x
♡ A Q 10 x x	♡ K x x x
◇ K x x x	◇ x x
♣ x x	♣ A K J x

OPENER	RESPONDER
1 heart	2 clubs
2 hearts	4 diamonds
4 hearts	Pass

Opener starts with his long suit because the short suit is lower-ranking. (If he opened one diamond and rebid two hearts he would be reversing, showing a strong opening, but he has a minimum.) Responder prepares to reverse into hearts by bidding clubs first. Opener rebids two hearts, instead of two diamonds, not for fear of being dropped in diamonds—the partnership is forced to two notrump or higher by the two-over-one response—but because partner is more likely to be interested in a five-card major suit than in a four-card minor. (This major-suit rebid is not rigidly limited, since it is under the forcing level and opener will get a chance to show his full strength later.) The two-heart rebid prevents responder from reversing with a three-heart jump—three hearts now would be merely a game try—so he uses the four-diamond convention to indicate that he would have reversed into hearts if he could. Opener now limits his hand by returning to the agreed-upon suit, and responder is content.

OPENER	RESPONDER
♠ Q x	♠ K J x x x x
♡ K Q x x	♡ x x
◇ A K J x	◇ x x x
♣ Q x x	♣ J x

OPENER	RESPONDER
1 heart	1 spade
2 notrump	3 clubs
3 diamonds	3 spades
Pass	

Opener does not quite have a one-club bid (he has 17 points, but two unsupported queens) so he opens the higher-ranking of his two four-card suits. (Observe that opener does not reverse by bidding diamonds first, even though he has a supermaximum in points. Reverses are not made with 4-4 hands; one diamond followed by two hearts shows a five-card heart suit.) Responder bids his suit, and opener shows as strong a balanced hand as the law allows by jumping to two notrump. Responder's three-club rebid is conventional, forcing opener to respond three diamonds—the fact that opener has a diamond suit is coincidental—and the three-spade bid after three clubs is an absolute sign-off which opener must respect.

ON DEFENSE AGAINST A ONE-DIAMOND,
ONE-HEART, OR ONE-SPADE OPENING BID

Very little deviation from standard defensive bidding is necessary when your Neapolitan opponents open one in a suit other than clubs. If anything you can afford to be a trifle more aggressive than usual, for you know that opener is not loaded with high cards. Do not enter the auction just because your opponent did not open one club, but resolve any doubtful action in favor of bidding.

Opener's tendency to bid a shorter suit before a longer will create new problems. You are likely to have the pattern for a takeout double of opener's longest suit, but he often will not be obliging enough to bid it right away. Therefore in this sort of sequence:

OPENER	YOU	RESPONDER	PARTNER
1 spade	Pass	1 notrump	Pass
2 hearts	*Double*		

you should treat the double as a takeout double of hearts, promising support for the other suits *including spades*. Remember the sort of suits that opener can bid, and you will realize that his opening bid may be in your side's best trump suit. Still, the delayed takeout double must be made at a fairly high level (this is one of the many advantages of the "canapé" style of bidding short suits first) so you must have solid values, not just suspicion, to act. A minimum hand for the double described earlier would be:

$$\spadesuit A Q 10 x \qquad \heartsuit x \qquad \diamondsuit A J x x \qquad \clubsuit K 10 x x$$

Another unusual situation that you may have to cope with is created by the "responder's reverse." Quite often, as we have seen, a two-over-one response is made in a short or false suit to prepare a reverse. So you should use a double of the first response at the *two level*:

OPENER	PARTNER	RESPONDER	YOU
1 spade	Pass	2 clubs	*Double*

to show that you have an overcall in clubs. Responder is planning to reverse into diamonds, hearts, or spades with a high bid, and it will then be too late to bid your suit. Of course, this means that you have to give up the takeout double of a two-over-one response. But this is no loss. If you have a balanced hand, even a very strong one, you are better off out of the auction—the opponents have more points than you; two-level responses are sound in Neapolitan bidding. If you have a freak two-suiter in the unbid suits—hearts and diamonds in the example auction—bid two notrump, the unusual notrump. This will show your distribution and will have more preëmptive effect than would a takeout double.

Last, use lead-directing penalty doubles of the few conventional bids described in this chapter. These are the artificial three-club bid by responder over opener's jump to two notrump, the forced three-diamond reply to it, and the four-diamond jump by responder to indicate a reverse.

III. Bidding a Hand with the Club Suit

Since the one-club opening bid is artificial, and no hand with fewer than 17 points qualifies, some method must be devised to bid hands that would otherwise be opened one club and now may not be. Your only suit may be clubs. You may have a long club suit and a second suit—here, of course, you can open in the higher-ranking suit and rebid in clubs, but this shows a minimum opening; what if you have a strong one?

The answer lies in the two specialized opening bids that show clubs in the Neapolitan System—one notrump and two clubs. These correspond roughly to the "minimum" and "strong" opening bids in the previous chapter: the two-club opening is "strong"—strong, remember, in distribution and playing strength, not primarily in points; the one notrump opening is "minimum"—from 13 up to 16, or conceivably 17, points in high cards, but usually with flat, unexciting distribution.

The one-notrump opening bid does not promise scattered honors in all suits, as it does in standard systems. You open one notrump when your only suit is clubs: 4-3-3-3 distribution with four clubs, 5-3-3-2 distribution with five clubs, 6-3-2-2 distribution with six clubs. Exceptionally, you may open one notrump with 4-4-3-2 distribution: four strong clubs and a worthless side suit, usually diamonds. These are one-notrump opening bids:

♠ x x x	♡ A K J	◇ x x x	♣ K Q J x
♠ K Q x	♡ x x	◇ J x x	♣ A K Q x x
♠ A x	♡ A x	◇ x x x	♣ K Q x x x x
♠ K x	♡ Q x x	◇ x x x x	♣ A K Q x

The two-club opening bid is usually a strong two-suited hand containing five clubs or more; opening two clubs is much like "reversing" into your long suit at the two level in the previous chapter (except that when you open two clubs partner does not yet know what your other suit is). You also open two clubs with a *one-suiter* in clubs that is unsuitable for a one-notrump opening—with a seven-card club suit or, conceivably, with a compact six-card club suit in a strong hand. These are two-club opening bids:

♠ x x	♡ K Q J x	◇ A x	♣ A Q 10 x x
♠ K Q 10 x x	♡ K x	◇ ——	♣ A 10 x x x x
♠ x x	♡ x	◇ A K Q 10 x	♣ K Q J x x
♠ A x	♡ K x	◇ x x	♣ K Q 10 x x x x

Other examples of opening bids are:

♠ x x	♡ x x x	◇ K x x	♣ A K Q J 10

Open one notrump. Never bid two clubs with 5-3-3-2 distribution.

♠ x x	♡ K x	◇ A J x	♣ A K J 10 x x

Open two clubs, for you have a magnificent suit and a "strong" opening. Normally, however, the 6-3-2-2 pattern is opened one notrump.

♠ K x x	♡ K 10 x x	◇ x	♣ A K x x x

Open one heart and rebid in clubs, showing a minimum hand and suggesting longer clubs than hearts. You are not strong enough to open two clubs. However, note this exception: When you have a four-card *spade* suit, you can lower the requirements for a two-club opening slightly; the example above would just barely qualify for two clubs if the hearts and spades were reversed.

There are two other exceptions to consider. First, you may hold 4-3-3-3 distribution with four clubs and a bare 12 or 13 points. In unfavorable vulnerability, one notrump may be too dangerous an opening bid. Of course, you are not compelled to open, but you should hate to pass a hand like:

♠ A x x   ♡ x x x   ◊ A x x   ♣ A x x x

particularly in third position. So open one diamond instead of one notrump. This promises a four-card suit at least, but partner will be forgiving.

Last, we come to the difficult 6-3-3-1 distribution, which falls into neither the one-notrump nor the two-club category—you have only a six-card club suit and no side suit; but you have a singleton, which makes one notrump an unattractive opening. Of course, if you have a "strong" hand:

♠ K x x   ♡ x   ◊ A x x   ♣ A K J x x x

there is no problem, you bid two clubs. With a minimum hand that has a strong singleton:

♠ Q 10 x   ♡ K   ◊ A Q x   ♣ K 10 x x x x

a one-notrump opening is surely superior. And there is a third option. With a hand like:

♠ x x x   ♡ x   ◊ K x x   ♣ A K J 10 x x

a three-club opening is best. As we will see later, the pre-emptive three-bid in *clubs* tends to be stronger than it is in any other suit. So with 6-3-3-1 distribution, pick the opening bid—one notrump, two clubs, or three clubs—that comes closest to describing your hand.

RESPONSES TO THE ONE-NOTRUMP OPENING

When partner opens one notrump, he has a somewhat balanced hand of 13 to 16 or 17 points. Therefore, if you want to play in notrump, you pass with 0 to 7 or 8 points, raise to two notrump with 10 or 11 points, and jump to three notrump with 12 points or more. However, since opener may well have two unstopped suits, the two-notrump and three-notrump responses should include stoppers in all suits.

The two-club response, taking opener into his real suit, is discouraging. You bid two clubs with almost any weak hand *

---

* With fewer than 4 points and club support, pass one notrump and run to two clubs after you are doubled.

that has three clubs or more and looks as if it will play better in the suit. You should also respond two clubs with many completely balanced hands of 9 to 11 points that are too weak for, or do not have the stoppers for, a raise to two notrump. Thus the two-club response is not a complete sign-off; opener will rebid with 15 points or more.

A jump to three clubs over the one-notrump opening is stronger—11 to 12 points or more—and forcing for one round. It denies the stoppers for a notrump raise and initiates a search for them at the three level.

Responses of two hearts and two spades are unlimited and forcing, like one-over-one responses; they show a minimum of 8 points with at least a four-card suit. In order to *sign off* at two hearts or two spades, you must first respond two diamonds. This forces opener to rebid two hearts; now you pass with hearts and bid two spades to sign off there. If you follow up your artificial two-diamond response with a rebid of *three* hearts or *three* spades, you are reversing into hearts or spades, forcing to game. Two diamonds followed by three diamonds shows a long diamond suit and no more than 11 or 12 points. Two diamonds followed by three clubs shows 10 to 12 points, a diamond suit, and club support.

Responses of three diamonds, three hearts, or three spades are jump shifts, showing the usual solid or semisolid suit and forcing to game at least.

THE DEVELOPMENT OF THE AUCTION

Sequences that follow the one-notrump opening bid are often characterized by a complicated series of bids searching out stoppers for three notrump. To understand them remember that opener has not promised honors in all suits or even in three suits; that opener's subsequent suit-bids show stoppers, not length, for he has no suit but clubs; that responder is likely to be looking for these stoppers when he does not bid a suit of his own (and sometimes even when he does).

After responder's jump to three notrump, opener will pass. If responder raises to two notrump, opener goes on to game with 15 points or more. With less he passes, or signs off with three clubs (a closing bid with a six-card suit).

When the response is two clubs, opener will pass with 14 points or fewer. If he has enough to rebid, he bids his stoppers—starting with the lowest-ranking suit he has stopped. Thus if opener rebids two diamonds, he has a diamond stopper and may have a stopper in either major suit (but not both);

if opener rebids two hearts, he has no diamond stopper but may have a spade stopper; if opener rebids two spades, he has only a spade stopper. And if opener rebids two notrump, he has stoppers in all three suits, and needs points from responder, not stoppers.

Responder's sign-off to all these bids is three clubs. Any other rebid requires about 9 points or more, for game is unlikely to be made with less, even opposite a maximum opener's hand. Responder will also sign off if it is obvious to him that a suit is unstopped. For example, this auction:

OPENER	RESPONDER
1 notrump	2 clubs
2 spades	

means that opener has no stopper in either hearts or diamonds. So responder signs off with three clubs, even with 11 points, if he cannot control both danger suits. For this auction, responder might hold:

♠ K x   ♡ J x   ◊ K Q J x   ♣ J x x x

If declarer has shown a stopper in the only suit responder was worried about, responder rebids two notrump with 9 points; three notrump with 10 or 11 points. However, responder may still be concerned about a suit higher-ranking than the one in which opener bid his stopper; opener may or may not have a stopper in a higher suit. So, if opener rebids two diamonds, and responder has one major stopped but is worried about the other, he bids the stopper he has; opener can sign off with three clubs if he does not have the fourth suit stopped, or bid two notrump or three notrump if he has. And if opener rebids two hearts, responder may have diamonds stopped but not spades; if so, he answers two spades! Opener will sign off with three clubs unless he has the spades stopped as well as the hearts.

Finally, if opener rebids two notrump over the two-club response, showing stoppers in diamonds, hearts, and spades, responder will sign off by bidding three clubs with fewer than 9 points. With enough strength to raise to three notrump, responder may check further (opener's stoppers are likely to be sketchy, for his strength is spread thin over many suits) by bidding three of his *weakest* suit. Opener can now bid three notrump, or sign off with four clubs.

Here are some typical auctions showing the hunt for stoppers:

OPENER	RESPONDER
♠ A K x	♠ Q x x
♡ x x x	♡ A J x
♢ x x	♢ x x
♣ A K J x x	♣ Q 10 x x x

OPENER	RESPONDER
1 notrump	2 clubs
2 spades	3 clubs
Pass	

OPENER	RESPONDER
♠ K 10 x	♠ Q J x
♡ Q x	♡ x x
♢ A Q x	♢ K x x
♣ K Q x x x	♣ A x x x x

OPENER	RESPONDER
1 notrump	2 clubs
2 notrump	3 hearts
4 clubs	Pass

OPENER	RESPONDER
♠ A J x	♠ 10 x x
♡ A x x	♡ K Q x
♢ x x x	♢ Q J x x
♣ A K 10 x	♣ Q x x

OPENER	RESPONDER
1 notrump	2 clubs
2 hearts	2 spades
3 notrump	Pass

Note that in all examples both opener and responder have close to maximum strength. With fewer than 15 points, opener would pass two clubs; with fewer than 9 points, responder would rebid three clubs regardless of stoppers.

When responder bids two hearts or two spades over one notrump, opener is forced to rebid. With a minimum, he rebids two notrump, or, with a long suit, three clubs. If responder now rebids his suit, opener will probably pass. If responder bids three in a suit lower-ranking than his first, he is inviting a preference or a search for stoppers—but opener may pass. If responder reverses with his rebid, he forces to

game; four clubs is a reverse into clubs. If responder rebids
three clubs, he shows club support and invites opener to bid
again—to show support for responder's first suit or to bid a
stopper to investigate notrump—but opener may pass.

Opener can show extra values over a two-heart or two-spade
response by bidding a suit. Again, he shows his lowest-ranking
stopper. Responder can now rebid his suit (discouraging),
show a stopper of his own, or bid notrump. Opener may also
raise responder's suit with a maximum and good three-card
support (it is known that he does not have four of any suit
but clubs).

After responder jumps to three clubs over one notrump,
opener starts a search for stoppers in the same fashion (one
level higher) as over a two-club response. If responder bids
the artificial two diamonds first and then three clubs or three
diamonds, opener may search for stoppers with a maximum or
pass with a minimum.

Here are some sample auctions:

OPENER	RESPONDER
♠ A Q x	♠ x x x
♡ x x	♡ K Q x
◇ x x	◇ A J x
♣ A Q x x x x	♣ K x x

OPENER	RESPONDER
1 notrump	3 clubs
3 spades	3 notrump
Pass	

Responder is strong enough to jump to three notrump over
one notrump; but spades may be wide open, so he forces with
three clubs instead. Opener shows his stopper (denying a
diamond or heart stopper) and responder cheerfully bids
game. Over a three-diamond rebid by opener, responder would
have bid three hearts ("I have the heart stopper, have you
anything in spades?") and over a three-heart rebid, responder
would have bid three spades ("I have the diamond stopper;
how about spades?")

OPENER	RESPONDER
♠ K x x	♠ Q J x x x
♡ Q x x	♡ K x
◇ J x x	◇ A x x x x
♣ A K J x	♣ x

OPENER	RESPONDER
1 notrump	2 spades
2 notrump	3 diamonds
3 spades	Pass

Responder, very much interested in game, forces with two of his higher-ranking suit. Opener rebids two notrump to show a balanced minimum. Responder cannot make game opposite a minimum, and his three-diamond rebid is looking for the best spot. When opener gives a preference, responder passes—opener would have raised directly (or bid a stopper) with a maximum.

OPENER	RESPONDER
♠ Q x x	♠ K J x x x x
♡ x x x	♡ K x
♢ A K x	♢ x x
♣ K J x x	♣ A Q x

OPENER	RESPONDER
1 notrump	2 diamonds
2 hearts	3 spades
4 spades	Pass

Responder's two-diamond bid is ambiguous and forces the two-heart reply. Responder now clarifies his first bid by "reversing" to three spades. Opener shows a minimum with support by raising; with a maximum he would bid a feature at the four level. Note that responder did not jump to three spades directly. This would promise a better suit.

OPENER	RESPONDER
♠ A x x	♠ J 10 x x x x
♡ x x	♡ Q x x
♢ K Q x	♢ x x
♣ A Q J x x	♣ K x

OPENER	RESPONDER
1 notrump	2 diamonds
2 hearts	2 spades
Pass	

Responder does not want to *force* with two spades; he wants to play there. So he bids two diamonds first, forces a two-heart reply, and then signs off. Opener has a maximum but has no option but to pass on this sequence.

If an opponent intervenes with an overcall over the one-notrump opening, all suit responses are natural and forcing. Notrump raises retain their usual meaning. Doubles are for penalties.

If the one-notrump opening is doubled, responder's only strong action is to redouble. Suit responses are rescues. If responder passes over the double, he has tolerance for the contract or a flat hand; opener should not rescue himself except into a long club suit.

RESPONDING TO THE TWO-CLUB OPENING BID

As responder, you should make a determined effort to bid over a two-club opening. It is not forcing, but it is strong and it often contains powerful distribution. So respond with 5 or 6 points but pass with less.

The raise to three clubs shows a weak hand, 5 to 9 points, with at least three-card support. Opener is free to pass, but he may also try for game by bidding his second suit, raising in clubs, or gambling on three notrump, according to his hand.

By far the most common response is two diamonds. This is a conventional, artificial bid, forcing for one round, and does not show any particular distribution or strength. It merely asks opener, "What is your second suit?" Opener replies by bidding his other suit, or by rebidding three clubs with the one-suited hand. (If opener's second suit is diamonds, he usually shows it not by bidding three diamonds, but by bidding two notrump.)

If responder has found a fit in the second suit, he can invite with a raise or jump to game. If he has not, he can sign off—usually by bidding three clubs. (If opener has replied three clubs, responder would then pass.) Responder's rebid of two spades over a two-heart rebid is likewise discouraging. If responder rebids three diamonds after his two-diamond bid, he wants to play the hand at three diamonds.

With greater strength, responder can rebid two notrump, a natural, encouraging bid, over opener's rebid at the two level. Or, he can bid a new major suit at the three level or jump to four clubs. All these actions force to game.

Let us see some examples of auctions that start two clubs—two diamonds.

OPENER	RESPONDER
♠ K Q x x	♠ J 10 x x
♡ x	♡ Q x x
◇ K x x	◇ Q x
♣ A K 10 x x	♣ Q x x x

OPENER	RESPONDER
2 clubs	2 diamonds
2 spades	3 spades
4 spades	Pass

Instead of raising clubs directly, responder looks for a major-suit fit. He finds it but can raise only to three with his minimum values. Opener has a little more than he promised (especially since he could open two clubs rather light with a secondary spade suit) and goes on to game. If one of his diamonds were a heart, he would pass.

OPENER	RESPONDER
♠ x	♠ J 10 x x
♡ A K x x x	♡ Q x x
◇ x	◇ Q x
♣ A J x x x x	♣ Q x x x

OPENER	RESPONDER
2 clubs	2 diamonds
2 hearts	3 clubs
3 hearts	4 hearts
Pass	

Here, responder has the same minimum but does not find a spade fit, so he signs off with three clubs, expecting this bid to end the auction. But opener shows his freak distribution by rebidding hearts, feeling that four clubs should be safe. And responder goes to game, valuing his two key queens properly.

OPENER	RESPONDER
♠ x x	♠ Q x x
♡ A K J x	♡ x x x
◇ x x	◇ K J x x x
♣ A K J x x	♣ x

OPENER	RESPONDER
2 clubs	2 diamonds
2 hearts	3 diamonds
Pass	

In the preceding example, opener respects the sign-off. He has shown all his values.

OPENER	RESPONDER
♠ A x	♠ Q 10 x
♡ x x	♡ K J x x
◇ x x	◇ A 10 x x
♣ A K J x x x x	♣ x x

OPENER	RESPONDER
2 clubs	2 diamonds
3 clubs	3 notrump
Pass	

Again, responder looks for a major-suit fit and does not find it. But he finds something just as good—a seven-card club suit (it could be a six-card suit, but then opener would have compensating values), so responder gambles on three notrump. Normally, 10 points will yield a good play for game opposite a two-club opening bid.

Responder can bid a good major suit of his own directly over the two-club opening. This is forcing, although not necessarily very strong. Opener will rebid just as he would over two diamonds: bidding a second suit if he has one (again, two notrump means diamonds) or three clubs with the one-suiter. If responder now rebids his suit, it is a sign-off.

Responder shows a "reverse" into clubs by making a two-heart or two-spade bid over two clubs (if necessary, "inventing" a suit) and then bidding four clubs at his next turn. This forces to game.

The two-notrump response to two clubs is constructive and forcing, showing 10 to 12 points and a balanced hand. The three-notrump response shows the same distribution and 13 or 14 points. But to jump to three notrump, responder needs secure stoppers in all three unbid suits.

Responder's jumps to three diamonds, three hearts, and three spades are the familiar jump shifts—forcing to game and promising solid or semisolid suits.

An overcall does not much alter the responses to the two-club opening. New-suit responses are natural and forcing; the three-club, two-notrump, and three-notrump responses retain their meaning. Obviously, the two-diamond convention can no longer be used.

A takeout double of two clubs does change the meaning of the responses a little, for responder's only strong action is to redouble. However, there is no need to rescue opener, who has a playable club suit, so new-suit bids, although nonforcing, are constructive, showing distributional values and no more than 11 points.

ON DEFENSE AGAINST TWO-CLUB
AND ONE-NOTRUMP OPENING BIDS

When your opponent opens with a Neapolitan two-club bid, caution must be exercised in coming into the auction. Opener has a strong hand, frequently containing a second suit, and you have to bid at the two level.

Overcalls should be very sound, indicating a strong suit and game ambition. With a strong suit and a strong hand in high cards as well, it is better to overcall than to double. Responder is in excellent position to raise clubs preëmptively over a takeout double, and you may find that you preëmptively over a takeout double, and you may find that you have to bid your suit at a prohibitive level.

The takeout double, then, should be used primarily on pattern—with good support for both major suits. If you have the majors you may score a game against a two-club opening, and in any event you can compete effectively for a partial. If you have diamonds you can overcall; if you have strong clubs, trap pass. The two-notrump overcall should be natural—a *very* powerful balanced hand, or a club stopper along with a long diamond suit.

The double of the artificial two-diamond response should be made to indicate a normal overcall in diamonds. You should not want to double for takeout with the majors, since responder almost surely has at least one four-card major for his two-diamond bid and opener is likely to hold a secondary major suit as well. However, the double of a two-heart or two-spade response should be for takeout; it should indicate a freak two-suiter in diamonds and the unbid major.

More problems are encountered when the opening bid is one notrump. The hand is far more likely to "belong" to your side for a game or partial, and the opponents may already be in serious trouble, ripe for a juicy penalty.

There are four elements in successful defense against the one-notrump opening bid: the "cue-bid" of two clubs for takeout; the penalty double; the overcall; and the pass. Let us consider each in turn.

The two-club overcall is an idle bid, for clubs is opener's

only suit. Therefore, it should be used as an artificial bid for a takeout, describing a primarily distributional hand and calling for partner to respond in a major suit. The more cards you have in the majors, the fewer points you need to overcall two clubs. Here are some sample two-club bids:

♠ A Q x x   ♡ K J x x   ◇ K x x   ♣ x x

♠ K J x x x   ♡ A Q x x   ◇ x x   ♣ x x

♠ A Q x x x   ♡ K J x x x   ◇ x x   ♣ x

♠ A K J x x   ♡ A Q 10 x x   ◇ x   ♣ x x

Partner should respond by bidding his better major (even a three-card suit—he is supporting *you*), and will bid diamonds only with no tolerance for either. He should *jump* in a four-card or longer major with 10 points or more. You will notice that the two-club takeout bid has a wide range—it describes patterns, not strength. The two-club bidder should raise the response with a maximum, pass the response (even if it is a jump) with a minimum. When the partner of the two-club bidder wishes to *insist* on game, he can jump to game, or cue-bid three clubs.

Note that the two-club takeout promises at least four cards in each major suit (exceptionally, you might have five spades and three hearts; if so, you will bid two spades over a two-heart response, suggesting tolerance for hearts but a preference for spades). With only one long major suit you can overcall. With a balanced hand too short in the majors, pass unless you are strong enough to double.

The double is primarily for penalties. (Partner should not take the double out with any balanced hand; but if he has freakish distribution, he may rescue into a suit at the two level with a weak hand or jump to the three level with a strong hand.) The penalty double should be made with either of two types of hand:

1. A strong, balanced hand of 15 points or more with good defense against clubs (usually three- or four-card length).
2. A strong hand containing a long suit that you can run against one notrump doubled.

When opening bidder's partner runs out of one notrump doubled into two clubs (his most common action with a bad hand), *your* partner should double with any three clubs and scattered values. You will then pass and lick your chops with type 1 hand, and take out to your long suit with type 2. When your partner is unable to double the two-club rescue, he should (unless he has freakish distribution) pass it around to you. *Your double has promised further action.* You will double with four trumps or take out to a suit. Actually, partner should pass *any* rescue bid around to you if he is unable to double himself. You can double with strong trumps or bid two notrump with type 1 hand, bid your suit with type 2.

When you double one notrump with the type 2 hand, be sure that your suit will run before theirs (clubs). You should have either the tops in your suit or enough club stoppers to give you time to set it up. Otherwise, jump in a strong suit over one notrump to show a big hand.

The non-jump overcall is limited by your failure to double one notrump or to jump. It indicates strong playing values— a husky suit, freakish distribution—but not a lot of points. Do not overcall with a 5-3-3-2 pattern and rarely with 5-4-2-2; there is not enough to gain and there is a lot to lose. One no-trump is a "weak" opening, but it may go as high as 16 or 17 points; and responder may be strong, and itching to double you.

Pass any hands that do not fit into any of the three categories above, even pretty good ones. Remember that a penalty double may commit you to bid again at a fairly high level. Pass any hand with five or more clubs; if you doubled and responder took out your double to two diamonds, two hearts, or two spades, you would not be able to rebid; if responder was going to run to two clubs over a double, he will do so anyway and *now* you can double for penalties.

When you pass any of these doubtful hands over the one-notrump opening—balanced hands of 14 points or less which do not have both majors; hands with 5-3-3-2 pattern but not strong enough to double; and hands with too many clubs— you are not passing the hand out. Your partner has not yet been heard from; he will probably act if the hand belongs to you.

In fourth seat (one notrump is opened on your *left,* partner passes) your action is greatly affected by the response. If opener's partner bids two hearts or higher, you should stay out of the auction unless you have a real freak—the enemy have many more points than your side has. But if responder passes, bids two clubs, or bids two diamonds, you may well decide to come in.

When the one-notrump opening is passed around to you, the two-club takeout bid is used exactly as it is in the direct position. The double is lightened to about 13 points and should most often be the balanced type hand, for you are not on lead. Therefore, the jump overcall should be employed with most strong unbalanced hands. And the simple overcall may be made, subject to vulnerability, on less freakish patterns; both opponents are limited, and opener cannot have four of your suit.

When responder bids two clubs over one notrump, you should really go out of your way to overcall. Both opponents are limited, but the limits are very wide. An overcall will disrupt the delicate search for stoppers and could well talk the opponents out of a game. And the hazy limits make it difficult for either of them to double you. Now, of course, the two-club takeout bid does not exist. You should double with either the strong balanced hand or the majors. Partner should respond in a major suit if he has one, but he should not strain to bid a three-card suit.

When responder bids two diamonds (the artificial response forcing opener to rebid two hearts) your double is for takeout, just as over two clubs. A lead-directing double would be futile here, for most of the time *you* will be on lead; in any case, you need the double for strong hands. Bid three diamonds to overcall in diamonds; this and other overcalls are normal, as if directly over the opening bid.

You may have many opportunities to make lead-directing doubles during those involved bidding sequences which search for stoppers. But remember who is on lead! If you are in second seat, over the opening bidder, do not double—you are on lead, and a double will only warn the opponent what lead to expect. If you are in fourth seat, behind responder, be alert to double any false suit that you want led; if you don't, partner will draw a negative inference and will surely lead something else. If you and your partner listen carefully to these auctions and make proper use of lead-directing penalty doubles, you should almost always be able to put up a maximum defense.

IV. Slam Bidding

Slam bidding in any system is merely an extension of its game
auctions, and Neapolitan slam bidding builds on the founda-
tions we have described in the previous chapters. Due to the
narrow limits within the various categories of opening bids,
one partner or the other is sure to know nearly the full potential of the hand before the third round of bidding. The early
sequences that suggest slam are these: a highly constructive
response to a one-club opening bid; opener's "strong" rebid
when responder himself is strong; responder's reverse when
opener has extra values; responder's jump shift.

When either partner diagnoses slam possibilities, he has
many varied tools to use in his investigation: cue-bids, the
Declarative-Informatory (D-I) four-notrump bid, Blackwood,
Gerber, asking bids, the five-notrump asking bid in trumps.
Let us examine each one.

Cue-bidding starts after a trump suit has been established
and the partnership is forced to game. This may be at a relatively low level, as in these auctions:

OPENER	RESPONDER		OPENER	RESPONDER
1 club	2 clubs		1 spade	2 diamonds
2 hearts	3 hearts		2 hearts	3 spades

OPENER	RESPONDER
1 diamond	2 hearts
3 hearts	

More often, it will be after game is reached. Any nonjump bid
in a suit other than the agreed-upon trump suit is a cue-bid.
It *shows* slam ambition and a control in the suit bid (usually
the ace or a void, occasionally the king or a singleton); it *asks*
partner for information about controls in other suits.

Partner can answer with a cue-bid, showing a control of his
own. Or, he may sign off by returning to the trump suit. Which
he does is determined by two factors—whether he can show
his control without getting too high; and whether he wishes
to encourage the slam investigation or discourage it. If he can
cue-bid an ace without getting the partnership a level higher,
he must do so. If cue-bidding his ace *would* increase the level,
he may do so or not at his option. Let us see how this works.

Suppose you open the bidding with one heart, holding:

♠ Q x x   ♡ K Q x x   ◇ A J x x   ♣ J x

Partner responds two clubs; you rebid two diamonds. Partner reverses to three hearts; you bid four hearts. Now partner cue-bids five clubs. You must cue-bid five diamonds even though you hate your hand, for this stays beneath the level of five hearts which you must reach regardless. But if your hand were:

♠ A x x   ♡ K Q x x   ◇ Q J x x   ♣ J x

you would sign off with five hearts. And if your jack of clubs here were the king, you would bid five spades even though it commits the partnership to slam, for now you should like your hand.

Here are some examples of slam investigation with cue-bids (it will be a good review of the previous chapters if you cover up the auctions and try to make each bid in turn):

OPENER	RESPONDER
♠ K J x	♠ A Q 10 x x x
♡ Q J x x	♡ x x
◇ A Q x	◇ K J x x
♣ K Q x	♣ A

OPENER	RESPONDER
1 club	2 diamonds
2 notrump	3 spades
3 notrump	4 diamonds
4 spades	5 clubs
5 diamonds	5 spades
Pass	

After responder shows five controls, opener rebids two no-trump to show his shape, not two hearts which would indicate a five-card suit. Responder shows his suit, and opener now limits his hand to a minimum by bidding three notrump, where he wants to play. Responder tries another suit (this four-diamond bid could be just a feature) and opener gives a preference to spades. Now responder cue-bids five clubs; opener must cue-bid five diamonds in return. And responder signs off; he has not found the heart control he was looking for.

OPENER	RESPONDER
♠ A Q x x	♠ K J 10 x x
♡ x x	♡ A x x
◇ x	◇ x x x
♣ A K J 10 x x	♣ Q x

OPENER	RESPONDER
2 clubs	2 spades
4 spades	5 hearts
6 spades	Pass

With a "strong" opening and long clubs, opener starts with
two clubs. Responder bids two spades, not two diamonds
(which asks for opener's second suit), since he might want to
play in spades even if opener cannot bid them. Opener jumps
to the game his hand guarantees. Now responder senses a slam
on "fit" and cue-bids his ace. Opener goes to slam, for he has
the diamond control that partner is worried about.

OPENER	RESPONDER
♠ A Q x x x	♠ K J x x
♡ A 10 x	♡ K Q x
◇ A 10 x	◇ K Q J x
♣ Q x	♣ x x

OPENER	RESPONDER
1 spade	2 diamonds
2 spades	4 diamonds
4 hearts	4 spades
5 diamonds	5 spades
Pass	

Responder prepares to reverse into spades by bidding diamonds first. Opener can safely rebid only two spades, since this
is forcing (below the two-notrump level). Responder can no
longer reverse by bidding three spades—it will now be a limited raise, so he uses the four-diamond convention. Spades are
now agreed upon, so opener can show his strength and probe
for slam by cue-bidding four hearts. Responder, with no aces
to show, signs off. Opener tries again by cue-bidding five
diamonds. But responder does not have the club control, and
the partnership stops short of the unmakable slam.

Note the one distinguishing feature of all these cue-bidding
auctions: There is one unbid suit that the cue-bidder cannot
control himself. If you are not worried about an unbid suit, do
not cue-bid—use the D-I four notrump instead.

Virtually all bids of four notrump *over four of a suit* (not jumps to four notrump, which are Blackwood) are the D-I four notrump, a convention similar to the old Culbertson 4-5 notrump. The four-notrump bidder shows certain values and asks partner to show *him* certain values. The four-notrump bidder shows:

1. Two aces at least, if he is the opening bidder (or has doubled or cue-bid over an opponent's opening) ; two aces at least, if he is the responder and has never made a limited bid; one ace at least, if he is the responder and *has* limited his hand.
2. At least a second-round control (king or singleton) in all unbid suits and in all *his* suits.

He asks partner to show him:

1. Controls or values in suits that partner has bid himself.
2. What partner thinks of the prospects for slam.

You can respond to this four-notrump bid in three different ways. First, you can sign off by returning to the agreed-upon trump suit (if no suit has been supported, consider that the agreed-upon suit is the last one bid—right before partner bid four notrump). Second, you can show a control or value in a suit *lower-ranking* than the trump suit; this is encouraging, but promises no extra strength since you have not committed the partnership to a slam. Third, you can make a positive response by showing a feature *higher in rank* than the trump suit. The strongest positive response of all is five notrump; this promises two aces and maximum strength for previous bidding. The jump to a slam in the agreed-upon suit is strongly positive also, but you are warning partner not to bid seven.

Suppose you have opened the bidding with one spade, holding:

♠ Q x x x   ♡ A J x x   ◇ K Q x   ♣ J x

Partner responds two clubs; you rebid two hearts. Partner bids four diamonds, showing a reverse into hearts; you sign off with four hearts. Now partner bids four notrump (D-I). What do you respond?

Sign off again with five hearts. You have a minimum, and partner probably has two losing spades. But if your hand were:

♠ K x x x   ♡ A J x x   ◇ K Q x   ♣ J x

you would bid five diamonds. You have a spade control, but dare not show it and commit the hand to slam, for you still have a minimum. Showing some values in diamonds is encouraging enough. With:

♠ A x x x   ♡ A J x x   ◊ K Q x   ♣ J x

bid five spades. Slam is sure, as you have close to a maximum and good controls in your suits. If your jack of hearts were the queen, you would bid five notrump.

Over the response, whether it was encouraging, discouraging, or positive, the four-notrump bidder can try for a grand slam by bidding five notrump. This shows one more ace than his four-notrump bid promised, and asks for partner's opinion about prospects for making seven. Partner can bid seven with a lot of plus values—solid suits, extra queens, king doubletons, etc.; he can encourage by showing some low-ranking feature, or he can sign off with six in the trump suit.

Let us see some slams bid with the D-I four notrump.

OPENER	RESPONDER
♠ A Q x	♠ K x
♡ A x x	♡ x x
◊ Q x x	◊ A K J 10 x x
♣ K 10 x x	♣ Q J x

OPENER	RESPONDER
1 notrump	3 diamonds
3 hearts	3 notrump
4 diamonds	4 notrump
5 spades	6 diamonds
Pass	

Opener must start with one notrump, as his only four-card suit is clubs; responder shows his nearly solid suit with a jump shift. Opener shows a feature (it cannot be a suit) and responder signs off with three notrump. Now opener shows his support, and responder comes to life with four notrump (D-I). (Note that he may bid four notrump with only one ace, since he has previously limited his hand. And observe that he controls the unbid spade suit.) Opener has close to a maximum, with controls in both suits he bid, so he makes a positive response and the slam is reached.

OPENER	RESPONDER
♠ K x x	♠ A x x x
♡ A K x	♡ x x
◊ A Q 10 x	◊ K J x x
♣ A Q x	♣ K x x

OPENER	RESPONDER
1 club	1 notrump
2 notrump	3 clubs
3 diamonds	4 diamonds
4 notrump	5 clubs
5 notrump	6 diamonds
Pass	

After responder shows four controls, opener rebids only two notrump—he has a lot of strength in reserve, but there is no hurry. Responder uses the three-club convention to find a suit fit and finds one. Responder's direct raise to four diamonds shows that he has little undisclosed value, but opener launches into four notrump (D-I). Responder is not willing to make a positive response (five spades) since he has close to a minimum for his previous bids, but he is not ashamed of his hand and encourages with five clubs. Opener now shows his extra ace and over-all power by rebidding five notrump (he knew after the first response that his side had all the aces and kings). But responder has bid every card he owns already, and signs off.

OPENER	RESPONDER
♠ A K x x x	♠ x
♡ A Q 10 x	♡ K J x x
◇ K x x	◇ A Q x x x
♣ x	♣ A x x

OPENER	RESPONDER
1 heart	2 diamonds
2 spades	3 hearts
4 diamonds	4 notrump
5 notrump	7 hearts
Pass	

Opener prepares to reverse into spades by bidding one heart; responder prepares to reverse into hearts by bidding two diamonds. And both follow through. Now opener cue-bids his diamond control and responder bids four notrump (D-I). Opener shows his maximum and two aces with five notrump, and responder happily goes to seven. The aces are accounted for, the diamond king has been cue-bid, and the heart queen is marked in opener's hand both by his reverse opening (showing good quality suits) and by his five notrump response to four notrump.

Most slams are reached through cue-bidding or use of the four notrump (D-I), but other devices are available for special hands. One of these is the Blackwood four-notrump bid. Four notrump is Blackwood when it is used over any bid of three notrump or lower. Raises in notrump to four notrump are not quantitative in the Neapolitan System, except in this one sequence:

OPENER	RESPONDER
1 spade [heart, diamond]	3 clubs
3 notrump	4 notrump

Four notrump is Blackwood, even over a four-level bid, whenever opener or responder uses it at his first or second turn to speak: one spade, four spades, four notrump; or four hearts, four notrump, etc.

Blackwood responses are the usual ones: five clubs = 0 or all four aces, five diamonds = one ace, five hearts = 2, five spades = 3. After a Blackwood four notrump, five notrump asks for kings. (If four notrump is D-I, five notrump is D-I; if four notrump is Blackwood, five notrump is Blackwood.)

Very rarely, four clubs (similar to "Gerber") is used to ask for aces, instead of the Blackwood four notrump. Four clubs asks for aces only when it is bid with a jump, and when it has no conceivable natural meaning. The responses are four diamonds = 0 or all four aces, four hearts = one ace, four spades = 2, four notrump = 3. After asking for aces with four clubs, the bidder may ask for kings with four notrump, or, if the ace-showing response was four notrump, with five clubs. Four clubs *never* asks for aces after a one-club opening.

Here is a Blackwood slam sequence:

OPENER	RESPONDER
♠ A 10 x	♠ K Q J x x
♡ K x x	♡ A Q x
◇ A 10 x x	◇ K Q J
♣ A J x	♣ K x

OPENER	RESPONDER
1 diamond	1 heart
2 notrump	4 notrump
5 spades	5 notrump
6 diamonds	7 notrump

Over the one-diamond opening (in the example on the preceding page), responder prepares to reverse into spades. But opener's jump to two notrump, showing the maximum balanced strength under a one-club opening, makes this unnecessary. Responder jumps to four notrump—Blackwood—for his only concern is the number of aces and kings opener has. Note that responder would never feel the need of a quantitative raise here—he knows almost surely that opener has exactly 16 points.

Another seldom-used device for slam bidding is the asking bid. This is a sudden, apparently useless jump in a previously unbid or clearly unplayable suit. It "asks" partner what control he has in that suit. Partner answers by "steps"—the next higher bid (as four hearts over four diamonds) shows least control, and each higher bid—each "step" skipped—shows more.

>1 step = no first or second-round control
>2 steps = the king or a singleton
>3 steps = the ace or a void
>4 steps = the ace and king

For example:

OPENER	RESPONDER
♠ A K Q 10 x x	♠ J x x x
♡ A	♡ x x x x
◇ A x x	◇ x
♣ K Q	♣ x x x x

OPENER	RESPONDER
1 club	1 diamond
1 spade	2 spades
4 diamonds	4 spades
6 spades	Pass

Opener rebids only one spade over the one-diamond negative response, for he is not quite willing to force to game (he intends to jump in spades next round). Responder must bid (one notrump has not been reached) and his raise shows four trumps and little else. Opener now makes the "useless" jump to four diamonds (spades have been agreed upon) as an asking bid. Responder skips one level to show his singleton—he cannot have a king—and opener bids the slam.

A *jump* to five notrump (when five notrump is bid without a jump it is just like the D-I four notrump except that it is looking for seven) is a specialized asking bid in the agreed-upon trump suit. It demands that partner bid a grand slam with a satisfactory trump holding or sign off at six otherwise.

When five notrump is bid by the original trump declarer:
1. If he has rebid his suit with a jump and has been supported, partner needs: Q-x or x-x-x-x.
2. If he has rebid his suit (no jump) and has been raised, partner needs: Q-x-x or x-x-x-x-x.
3. If he has not rebid his suit until raised, partner needs four trumps headed by two of the three top honors.

When five notrump is bid by partner of the original trump declarer:
1. If declarer has rebid his suit and has been supported, declarer needs: five trumps headed by two of the three top honors.
2. If declarer has not rebid his suit until supported, declarer needs: four trumps headed by two of the three top honors.

An example:

OPENER	RESPONDER
♠ K Q x	♠ A x
♡ A 10 9 x	♡ K J x x
◊ K J x x	◊ A x
♣ x x	♣ A K Q x x

OPENER	RESPONDER
1 heart	2 clubs
2 diamonds	3 hearts
4 hearts	5 notrump
6 hearts	Pass

Responder reverses into hearts in order to set the trump suit, and then jumps to five notrump to check on its quality. Opener's holding is insufficient, so he signs off.

To check on trump quality for a *small* slam, raise to five in the agreed-upon major suit. Trumps must be your only concern, since you have used none of the many methods for checking on other features. Partner will pass without undisclosed values in trumps.

V. Preëmptive Opening Bids

The Neapolitan System offers a wide range of preëmptive
openings. These are: the opening three-bid in a suit; the two-
notrump opening; the three-notrump opening; four- and five-
bids in suits; and weak two-bids in diamonds, hearts, or spades.

The three-bids, particularly, have narrower limits than in
standard methods. Opening bids of three diamonds, three
hearts, and three spades are *not* made with fairly good hands,
just under the strength for a one-bid. They describe long suits
missing top honors, in hands that are nearly worthless defen-
sively. The minimum playing strength must, of course, be
determined by the vulnerability. These are typical three-bids,
nonvulnerable:

1. ♠ Q J 10 x x x   ♡ x x   ◇ x   ♣ Q x x x
2. ♠ x   ♡ A 10 9 x x x x   ◇ x x x   ♣ x x
3. ♠ K x   ♡ x   ◇ K J 10 x x x x ♣ x x x

Vulnerable, you would want an extra trump, or at least an
additional honor in trumps, to preëmpt.

Clearly, the normal response to a three-bid is "Pass." However, responder may raise with a powerful hand, or preëmptively. If he bids three notrump, he wants to play there. (Three
notrump should almost never be bid over three hearts or three
spades, for the suits are unlikely to "run," but may be bid over
three diamonds. So do not open three diamonds with quite
such trashy suits as you would open three hearts or three
spades.)

A new-suit response to a three-bid is a one-round force.
Opener answers by bidding a side honor (three notrump shows
an honor in *responder's* suit, doubleton at least) or by rebidding his suit. With hand 3 above, the three-diamond opener
would bid three spades over a three-heart response, or three
notrump over a three-spade response.

The preëmptive bid that shows a solid or semisolid suit is
two notrump. (All strong hands are opened one club, remember.) To open two notrump, you must have a seven-card diamond, heart or spade suit, headed by the ace and king or by
the ace-queen-jack, with no side honors. These are two-
notrump opening bids:

♠ A K Q x x x x   ♡ x   ◇ x x   ♣ x x x

♠ x x   ♡ A Q J 10 x x x   ◇ x x   ♣ x x

♠ x   ♡ x x   ◇ A K J x x x x   ♣ x x x

Over the two-notrump opening, responder *must* bid three clubs, and opener completes the picture of his hand by showing his suit. Responder now places the contract, or forces with a bid in a new suit. (Tend to avoid the two-notrump opening when you have a diamond suit; notrump may play from the wrong side.)

The opening bid of three clubs resembles the two-notrump opening more than it does the other three-bids. It shows a six- or seven-card suit with top cards, and it may be the strength of a minimum opening bid (when the hand is unsuitable for a one-notrump opening and too weak for two clubs). These are three-club openings:

♠ x x   ♡ x x   ◇ x x   ♣ A K J 10 x x x

♠ x x   ♡ x   ◇ Q x x x   ♣ A K Q J x x

The second example could be opened one diamond (but not two clubs; it is too weak); however, three clubs is more descriptive.

Responses to the three-club opening are the same as for other three-bids, and call for identical rebids.

With greater playing strength (eight-card suits, freakish distribution) opener may preëmpt with a four-bid in any suit, or even with five in a minor. These bids are the same as in standard systems.

The opening bid of three notrump is not needed for strong hands, so it is a gambling bid. Opener has a long, solid minor suit with two honors on the side. For example:

♠ Q x   ♡ K x   ◇ A K Q J x x x   ♣ x x

Responder will pass with a smattering of cards or a sporting disposition. Otherwise, he may run out to four clubs, and opener will pass with a club suit, or bid four diamonds with diamonds. When responder wants to play in a minor suit *game,* he bids five clubs; and again opener passes or bids diamonds. Any other suit response is a force.

Opening two-bids are weak, except for two clubs (which shows the "strong" opening bid and a club suit). Two diamonds, two hearts, and two spades are very much like the weak two-bids used in the United States—one-suited hands just under the strength for an opening bid, with good six-card suits:

♠ A J 10 x x x   ♥ K J x   ♦ x x x   ♣ x

♠ A K x   ♥ Q J 10 x x x   ♦ x x   ♣ x x

The first example is a minimum, the second a maximum weak two-bid.

Responses in new suits are forcing for one round; rebids are analogous to those after opening three-bids.

When partner has passed, you may preëmpt with three or four in any suit with considerably better hands—even up to the strength of a minimum opening bid—for you are no longer afraid of missing game or slam. Fourth-hand three-bids are, of course, mildly invitational, but the suit should not meet the requirements for a two-notrump opening. Fourth-hand two-notrump openings may have honors on the side; you can open two notrump and jump to four in a major over the forced three-club reply (instead of opening four hearts or four spades initially) to give partner the option of looking for slam.

New-suit responses by a passed hand are natural and non-forcing. Responder wants to play in *his* suit, not in opener's.

ON DEFENSE AGAINST PREËMPTIVE OPENINGS

Playing against the Neapolitan System, your defense against opening preëmptive bids should be much the same as it is normally. First- or second-hand three-diamond, three-heart and three-spade openings are weaker than in standard practice, but don't enter the auction or stretch to game or slam entirely on that account—opener's partner has not been heard from. However, your hands will frequently take about one trick more on offense than their points warrant, for almost all the defensive strength is massed in one hand and you know it. So if you are on the borderline between a bid and a pass, bid.

The artificial two-notrump opening gives you the opportunity for very accurate defensive bidding. You have two choices: to double two notrump directly, or to wait for responder's three-club bid and opener's reply and *then* double opener's suit. The immediate double of two notrump should be made with solid high-card values, while the delayed double is primarily distributional: a "pattern" takeout double of opener's suit. Thus, with:

♠ A K x   ♡ x x   ◇ A Q 10 x   ♣ K Q x x
♠ K Q x x   ♡ ——   ◇ Q J 10 x x   ♣ K Q x x

double directly with the first hand; with the second, wait until opener bids three hearts and *then* double. The dividing line should be 15 to 16 points in high cards; and the delayed takeout double should guarantee four-card or better support in the "other major."

Overcalls should show strong suits, good distribution, and some defensive values. With 15 or more points in high cards, double two notrump directly even if you have a strong suit; then bid your suit after opener bids his. And with no defensive strength, when you are looking primarily for a sacrifice, warn partner by *passing* over two notrump and overcalling later.

In fourth seat, with two notrump opened on your left and three clubs bid on your right, the defense is much the same. Double three clubs immediately with any hand rich in high cards, and wait to double the suit with primarily distributional values.

You should also have a specific defense against the gambling opening bid of three notrump. Again, double with a defensive hand containing substantial high-card values (or with a running suit). When you have an offensive type of hand with support for both majors, bid your better minor suit (the one you think is not opener's solid suit) for takeout. For example, with:

♠ K Q J x x   ♡ A Q 10 x   ◇ K Q x   ♣ x

bid four diamonds over the three-notrump opening. Partner will bid his better major suit or, conceivably, pass. Do not double three notrump with this type of hand. The opponent may make three notrump doubled when you could make game in a major.

VI. Defensive Bidding

When an auction starts with an opponent's opening bid, the Neapolitan System handles it in very nearly standard fashion. Overcalls are limited in strength; the takeout double is the principal defensive weapon with good hands; one-notrump overcalls, jump overcalls, and cue-bids in the opponent's suit are all normal strong bids. There are differences in precise re-

quirements, responses, and style, but the general approach is
the same as in ordinary systems.

Why are there so few differences? *Offensive* bidding (when
your side has opened) in the Neapolitan System is geared to
the artificial one-club opening bid, but *defensive* bidding does
not have the artificial foundation. In fact, it is perfectly practi-
cal to play the whole system but to use your customary defensive methods. This chapter will concentrate on those aspects in
which the Neapolitan style differs from standard practice.

Overcalls are made on a wide range of hands containing
from 6 points (with a long suit) up to the strength of a minimum opening bid. The chief variation from standard bidding
is in the quality of the suits that can be bid: At the one level,
virtually any four-card suit headed by a high honor may serve
for an overcall. The Neapolitan style is to overcall at the one
level if possible, even concealing a longer suit that would
have to be bid at the two level. Thus, with:

♠ Q x x x   ♡ x x x   ◇ x   ♣ A Q J 10 x

overcall a one-diamond opening bid with one spade. Of
course, with two suits that can be bid at the one level, or if
both must be bid at the two level, bid the longer first; and if
they are equally long, bid the higher-ranking first.

Partner's raise of your one-level overcall is only mildly invitational; it is largely preëmptive. His *jump* raise is a strong
invitation but is nonforcing. Any new suit he bids is an overcall of his own, and nonforcing. To force, partner must cue-
bid the last suit bid by the opponents.

The *jump* overcall shows a hand of about the strength of a
minimum opening bid, largely concentrated in one suit. For
example, with:

♠ A K J 10 x x   ♡ x x   ◇ A x x   ♣ x x

jump to two spades over an opponent's one-bid. This is invitational but nonforcing; with much more you would double
instead. A new suit bid by partner over your jump overcall is
progressive, but nonforcing.

The one-notrump overcall is normal, showing 16 to 18
points and a balanced hand. Partner can check for a major suit
with the two-club (Stayman) convention.

The immediate cue-bid of opener's suit is forcing to game,
and promises first- or second-round control of that suit. But
two clubs over one club is just an overcall.

THE TAKEOUT DOUBLE

With the three exceptions noted above, a strong hand calls for a takeout double. A minimum opening bid is the least you should have to double; and your strength is limited only by your failure to cue-bid and force to game directly.

It is in responding to the takeout double that the differences start. Neapolitan System players use the "Herbert Convention," in which the response of the next-higher bid is negative and artificial. Thus, in response to partner's takeout double of one club, your bid of one diamond is simply a denial and does not show diamonds. The same is true of one heart over one diamond doubled; one spade over one heart doubled; one notrump over one spade doubled; etc. You use the artificial denial when you have a very bad hand with no five-card suit that you can bid at the one level; or when you have fewer than 5 points and would otherwise have to bid a four- or five-card suit at the two level. Suppose partner has doubled a one-diamond opening bid. You should respond one heart with either of these hands:

♠ J x x   ♡ x x x   ◇ J x x x   ♣ x x

♠ K x x   ♡ x x x   ◇ J x   ♣ 10 x x x x

However, on the same auction do *not* bid one heart with any of these hands:

1. ♠ Q J x x x   ♡ x x x   ◇ x x x   ♣ x x
2. ♠ K Q x x   ♡ x x x   ◇ x x x x   ♣ x x
3. ♠ K x x   ♡ x x x   ◇ x x   ♣ Q 10 x x x

You may bid one spade with Hand 1, since you have a five-card suit to show at the one level. You may bid one spade with Hand 2, because you have a little something and can bid at the one level. You may bid two clubs with Hand 3, for you have the required 5 points to go to the two level in a five-card suit.

You may make a positive response with about 5 to 9 points. (To make a positive response in the next-higher suit, the denial suit, jump in it.) You may jump in your suit (or double-jump in the denial suit) with 9 to 10 points or more; this is a one-round force. A cue-bid of the opponent's suit forces to game.

Doubler shows extra strength when he bids a new suit over your response (even over a denial). His raises are invitational.

If he bids the opponent's suit after doubling it, he shows
length in that suit and a willingness to play there.

Neapolitan defense against opponents' preëmptive openings
varies according to the bid which is made. Over all opening
four-bids, a double is optional, and four notrump is for takeout. Defense against three-bids depends on the suit opened:

Over three hearts or three spades:	The *double* is optional and guarantees support for the unbid major suit. Three notrump is for takeout and denies support for the other major.
Over three diamonds:	The *double* is optional. Three notrump is for takeout, but shows tolerance for notrump play.
Over three clubs:	The *double* is for penalties. Three diamonds is for takeout, primarily in a major, but partner may pass. Three notrump is natural, to play there.

Weak two-bids are treated like three-bids, with the same
defense one level lower. But two notrump over two diamonds
does not show tolerance for notrump; it is strictly for takeout.

Last, there is the specialized two-notrump overcall for two-
suited hands. If the opponents have bid two suits, your two-
notrump overcall (whether or not it is a jump) shows at least
five cards in each of the other two suits. If the opponents have
bid only one suit (as when you jump to two notrump over an
opening bid, or when the opening bid is raised and you overcall with two notrump) you show at least five cards in each
of the two lowest-ranking unbid suits. Thus, a two-notrump
bid over a one-heart or one-spade opening shows diamonds and
clubs; over one diamond or one club it shows hearts and the
unbid minor.

VII. Summary of the Neapolitan Club System

Following is a recapitulation, in outline form, of all the material covered.

NOTE: In recent years, the Neapolitan Club System has undergone some changes to improve it and make it more "natural." These changes are included without comment in the text of this book. In the Summary, however, those aspects which differ from previous practice are marked with asterisks (*).

OPENING BIDS

Open one club
with 17 to 18 high-card points or more. With less, you may
Open one diamond, one heart, one spade:
If you have only one suit, bid it, regardless of quality.
If you have two suits of equal length, bid the higher-ranking first.
If you have two suits of unequal length, bid the shorter first.
EXCEPTION: if your short suit is lower in rank, and you have a minimum hand, bid the long suit first.

Open one notrump
when your only suit is clubs. You need not have stoppers. But

Open two clubs
with seven clubs or more; with six clubs and maximum strength; with five clubs or more, maximum strength, and a side suit.

RESPONSES, REBIDS, AND DEVELOPMENT

When the opening bid was one club:
Responder shows his controls (aces and kings) by steps; opponent's interference changes the step system.
The auction must proceed to one notrump or higher. If responder shows two controls, the partnership is forced to two notrump. Any higher response forces to game.

If opener's rebid is a jump in a suit, he forces to game.
With less, opener bids his suits in order of length and rank, but may distort his distribution to stay at the one level, or bid a lower-ranking four-card suit rather than a higher.

Responder shows his best suit with his first rebid. Next, he bids features of his hand to encourage; to sign off; he raises opener, bids notrump or passes.

If opener's rebid is in notrump:
Responder can use two clubs over one notrump to check for majors;
Responder can use three clubs over two notrump to find any four-card fit;
Responder can show long suits of his own.

When the opening bid was one diamond, one heart, one spade:

Responder passes with 0 to 4 or 5 points.
He should bid any suit at the one level rather than respond one notrump.
He needs 10 points to bid a new suit at the two level. This forces the partnership to two notrump, unless responder gives a preference.*
He raises opener's suit with 5 to 9 or 10 points.
He jump-raises with 9 to 12 points (nonforcing).
He answers one notrump with 5 to 10 points, with no suit to bid at the one level.
He jumps to two notrump with 11 or 12 points, all unbid suits stopped, balanced hand.
He jumps to three notrump with 13 to 15 points, all unbid suits stopped, balanced hand.
He jumps in a new suit with 13 points or more and a semi-solid suit (clubs may be a weaker suit).
He normally shows a game-going hand by reversing. The first suit may be false. Four-diamond conventional rebid shows reverse into opener's suit when opener's rebid inhibits natural reverse. After one-spade response to one-heart opening, four diamonds shows reverse into hearts.*
He bids freely over opponent's overcalls, just as above.*
He redoubles or jumps to two notrump over opponent's takeout double with any strong hand. All other bids, even jumps, are limited.

Opener has two types of rebid:
"Strong"—14 to 16 points, good distribution, honors in long suits—
If he bids a second suit, higher-ranking than the first,* at the two-level.

If he jumps in a lower-ranking suit. The second suit is at least as long as the first.

If he jumps in his first suit.

If he jumps in responder's suit.

"Minimum"—flat distribution, or weak suits, or less than 14 points—

If he bids a second suit lower-ranking than his first. The second suit is probably longer, but may even be shorter than the first.

If he raises responder's suit.

If he rebids one notrump or two notrump—the latter with 16 or 17 points, but flat.

If he rebids his suit. However, after a two-over-one response the rebid of a major suit is unlimited.

Responder's only forcing rebid is a reverse.

New suits, raises and jumps are invitational.

Rebid of three clubs after opener's jump to two notrump is conventional. Opener must rebid three diamonds and responder signs off. Other new suits are forcing; responder's rebid of his first suit is invitational.

When the opening bid was one notrump:

Responder passes 0 to 8 points with a hand suitable for notrump play.

He bids two clubs with three-card or longer support and 5 to 10 points.

He bids two diamonds,* forcing a two-heart rebid, to sign off at two hearts or two spades, or to reverse into three hearts or three spades.

He bids two hearts or two spades, forcing for one round, with long suits.

He bids two notrump with 10 or 11 points and stoppers in diamonds, hearts, and spades.

He bids three notrump with 12 points or more and stoppers in diamonds, hearts, and spades.

He forces with three clubs with 12 points or more and three or more clubs.

He jumps to three diamonds, three hearts, or three spades, with semisolid suits. Game force.

Opener, over two clubs, passes with 13 or 14 points. With 15 to 17 points, he bids his lowest-ranking stopper, or he bids two notrump with stoppers in diamonds, hearts, and spades.

Over two diamonds, he must bid two hearts.

Over two hearts or two spades, he may sign off with two notrump or three clubs, or may encourage by raising or by bidding his lowest stopper.

Over three clubs, he bids his lowest stopper or three notrump with diamonds, hearts and spades stopped.

Responder, after he has first bid two clubs, signs off with three clubs holding 9 points or less or if he knows that a suit is unstopped. Holding 9 to 11 points, he can rebid two notrump or three notrump or show a stopper.

After first bidding two diamonds, two hearts or two spades he can force only with a reverse.

When the opening bid was two clubs:

Responder passes with 0 to 5 points.

He bids two diamonds, conventional, to locate opener's second suit.

He forces with two hearts or two spades, showing a good suit.

He bids two notrump (10 or 11 points) or three notrump (12 points or more) holding a balanced hand with stoppers.

He raises to three clubs with 5 to 9 points and three-card support at least.

He jumps to three diamonds, three hearts or three spades with a semisolid suit. Game force.

Opener, over two diamonds, shows his second suit (two notrump means diamonds) or rebids clubs.

Over two hearts or two spades, he bids his second suit (two notrump means diamonds) or rebids clubs.

Over two notrump, he bids his second suit, rebids clubs, or raises to three notrump.

Over three clubs, he passes or rebids according to his strength.

Responder, after he has first bid two diamonds,* signs off in clubs or diamonds, raises opener's second suit, or forces with a new suit at the three-level.

After he has first bid two hearts or two spades, signs off with a rebid in the same suit, or forces with a new suit.

THE ROMAN CLUB SYSTEM

The original of this system must be credited to Giorgio Manca of Rome, who formulated most of its principles and structure. In Italy's three World Championship victories, this system was played by Giorgio Belladonna and Walter Avarelli, who, along with others, helped perfect and codify the Roman Club system.

The basic theory of Roman Club bidding is that the opening bid shows the distributional pattern of the hand.

There are differing opening bids for balanced hands, for hands containing long suits, and for three-suited hands.

Holding 4-3-3-3 or 4-4-3-2 distribution:
> One club is opened with 12 to 16 points or with 21 to 26 points.
> One notrump is opened with 17 to 20 points.

Holding 5-4-4-0 or 4-4-4-1 distribution:
> Two clubs is opened with 12 to 16 points.
> Two diamonds is opened with 17 or more points.

Holding a suit of five cards or longer:
> One diamond, heart or spade is opened with almost all 12-point or better hands, but—
> Two hearts, spades or notrump is opened with hands containing two suits one of which is a club suit shorter than, or as long as, the side suit.
> One club is opened with a one-suited or two-suited hand that has ten or more winners.
> Three, four or five in a suit is opened with hands containing a very long suit that has three of the four top honors. No outside strength may be held, and opener announces enough playing strength to hold a set to 500 points.

I. The One-Club Opening Bid

The opening bid of one club in the Roman System is artificial and forcing. Most often, though, it describes not a strong hand, as in the Neapolitan System, but a balanced minimum opening of 12 to 16 points. However, it is a three-way bid, for if the opening one-club bidder jumps in a suit with his rebid, he has a standard, forcing-to-game two-bid; and if he jumps in notrump, he has a standard two-notrump or three-notrump opening bid. These are all opening bids of one club:

Type 1: ♠ K Q J x   ♡ A Q J x   ◇ x x x   ♣ x x

Type 2: ♠ A K J 10 x x   ♡ A K J x x   ◇ K x   ♣ ——

Type 3: ♠ K x   ♡ A Q x   ◇ K Q x x   ♣ A K Q x

    Obviously, the one-club opening bid is based on a Type 1 hand nine times out of ten; but the tenth time, opener will rebid with a suit jump to indicate Type 2 or with a notrump jump to show Type 3.

    When you have 4-3-3-3 or 4-4-3-2 distribution (no five-card suit, no singleton) and 12 to 16 points, there is no choice of opening bids in the Roman System. You must open one club. Of course, you always have the option of passing a bare 12-point hand, particularly when vulnerable. But you may not open in any other way. And you may not open one club without these distributional and point-count requirements, unless you are prepared to jump with your rebid to show Type 2 or Type 3. You do *not* open one club with any of these hands:

♠ Q J x x   ♡ K x   ◇ x   ♣ A K J x x x

♠ K x   ♡ A x x   ◇ A x x   ♣ Q J 10 x x

♠ K x   ♡ x   ◇ K x x   ♣ A Q 10 x x x x

    The only hands that may be opened one club when they contain five-card suits * or singletons are standard forcing two-bids, and these examples fall far short. As we will see later, other sequences are provided to handle the example hands.

---

   * It is not absolutely forbidden to open 5-3-3-2 hands of 12 to 16 points with one club, but it should almost never be done. The fact that your choice of opening bid indicates your distribution is the cornerstone of the Roman System. In all the World Championship matches, only once did a Roman player open one club with a five-card suit. He held

    ♠ K 10 9   ♡ 9 6 4   ◇ Q 8   ♣ A Q J 5 3

RESPONDING TO ONE CLUB

When partner opens one club, you have no way of knowing which type of hand he holds, but this makes no difference in your first response. You proceed to describe your hand to him under the assumption that he has a balanced minimum, and he will let you know with his rebid if he has Type 2 or 3. There are three main classes of response, graded according to strength: negative responses, constructive responses, and strong responses.

The negative response to a one-club opening bid is one diamond. You answer one diamond whenever you have 7 points or fewer, and with occasional slightly stronger hands that are unsuitable for a constructive response. With all these hands:

1. ♠ x x x ♡ x x x ◇ x x x ♣ x x x x
2. ♠ K Q x x ♡ x x x ◇ x x x ♣ Q x x
3. ♠ x x ♡ x x ◇ Q x x ♣ K 10 9 x x x

bid one diamond over one club. You may not pass with Hand 1—one club is forcing. You may not respond in a suit or "raise" clubs with Hands 2 and 3, because you lack the required point-count.

Constructive responses are made with hands of 8 to 11 points. However, you may shade your response by a point or two if you have a long suit, particularly a five- or six-card major. Any nonjump takeout in a suit—one heart, one spade, two clubs—is constructive, and two diamonds is considered merely constructive also, for it is the minimum available diamond bid (one diamond is the artificial negative response). In this 8-to-11-point range, these are the rules for choosing your response:

1. Bid any four-card or longer major suit, preferring it to a longer minor suit.

2. If you have two four-card major suits, bid hearts, allowing opener room to bid spades.

3. With five hearts and five spades, bid hearts and rebid in spades. With five diamonds and five clubs, bid diamonds first. With five in a major and five in a minor, bid and rebid the major.

4. Bid a minor suit when you have no four-card or longer major. But two-club and two-diamond responses require 9 points and at least a five-card suit.

Therefore, if partner opens one club and you hold:

♠ J x x x　　♡ A x　　◇ x x　　♣ K 10 x x x

respond one spade. You have enough for a constructive response; and prefer the major to the minor.

♠ A K x x　　♡ Q x x x　　◇ x x　　♣ J x x

Respond one heart. With two four-card majors, bid hearts.

♠ x x x　　♡ A x x　　◇ A J 10 x x　　♣ x x

Respond two diamonds. You have the required points and a five-card suit, and do not want to make the negative *one*-diamond reply.

♠ Q x x　　♡ K x x　　◇ x x x　　♣ K 10 x x

Respond one diamond. You have 8 points, enough for a constructive response, but you have no suit to bid at the one level and you would require 9 points, and a better suit, to go to the two level. Always resolve any doubt in favor of making the negative response.

The strong responses require 12 points or more, and are these:

　One notrump, showing 12 to 15 points with nearly balanced distribution (4-3-3-3, 4-4-3-2, 5-3-3-2).

　Two notrump, showing 16 points or more and similar distribution.

　Two hearts or two spades, promising a five-card or longer suit headed by two of the three top honors.

You will notice that many two-suited hands fall into none of the three categories. With these hands you first bid your shorter suit and next bid your longer suit (with a jump of one it is necessary to force declarer). This will indicate that your first response was "strong," not merely constructive.

　With two five-card suits:

　Clubs and diamonds: bid clubs first, then diamonds.

　Spades and hearts: jump in the stronger suit, then bid the other if necessary.

　A major and a minor: bid the minor, then the major.

Here are the first examples of the "canapé" style of bidding the longer suit *after* the shorter. In most sequences in the Roman System, when a player bids two suits, the second suit is the longer one.

Partner opens one club. What should your response be, holding:

♠ A K J x x   ♥ A x x   ♦ x x x   ♣ J x

Bid two spades. You have the required point-count and suit for this strong response.

♠ K J x x x   ♥ Q x x   ♦ A K x   ♣ x x

Bid one notrump. You have even distribution and are within the 12-to-15-point range. You may not jump in spades without A-K, A-Q, or K-Q.

♠ A J x x x   ♥ x   ♦ A Q x   ♣ Q x x x

Bid two clubs. You intend to rebid in spades, showing long spades, shorter clubs, and a strong response. Your suit is too weak for two spades, your distribution is unsuitable for no-trump. Note that you can bid a minor ahead of a major when you are strong enough to bid both.

♠ x x   ♥ K Q x   ♦ A K J x x   ♣ K x x

Bid two notrump. You meet the 16-point requirement and have even distribution.

In addition to the normal responses discussed above, there are available certain preëmptive actions. Responder can jump to four hearts or four spades with a six- or seven-card suit headed by the A-K, or by the K-Q-J, with a little outside value. Bid four spades over one club with:

♠ A K 10 9 x x x   ♥ Q x x   ♦ x x   ♣ x

Responder can jump to three hearts, three spades, four clubs or four diamonds with a poor hand and a six- or seven-card suit. (Opener might raise the major preëmpts to game with a magnificent maximum, but generally should pass.) Responder may hold, to bid three hearts over one club:

♠ x   ♥ K J 10 x x x x   ♦ J x x   ♣ x x

Finally, responder can jump to three clubs or three diamonds to describe a semi-solid six- or seven-card suit headed by A-K-Q or at least A-K-J. Opener uses his judgment in placing the final contract.

OPENER'S REBIDS AND DEVELOPMENT
OF THE AUCTION

Opener's rebids vary according to the nature of the response. When responder has answered with the negative one diamond, opener moves cautiously to find a playable spot at the one level. If he has a four-card major, he bids it (with both majors, he bids hearts); without a four-card major, he will bid a three-card heart suit; with two four-card minors he can rebid one notrump, but he should tend to avoid this rebid unless he has a maximum, for one notrump is very easy to double for penalties and responder may have nothing at all.

At his second turn, the one-diamond responder must bid the full value of his hand forthwith, for opener is likely to pass any rebid. Responder should pass opener's second bid if he has a worthless hand (but should show any four-card spade suit at the one level). He may raise opener's suit with four-card or longer support and 6 to 7 points; he may even jump-raise, with excellent distributional support. He can bid a suit of his own—conceivably with a jump, if his distribution is freakish. In short, having limited his hand with the one-diamond response, he is now free to do whatever he wants, but no rebid he makes is more than slightly invitational, for game is most unlikely.

Here are some examples of how the auction develops after the opening bid of one club and the negative response of one diamond:

OPENER	RESPONDER
♠ A x x	♠ K J x x
♡ K x x	♡ x x
◇ K Q x x	◇ x x x
♣ Q x x	♣ 10 x x x

OPENER	RESPONDER
1 club	1 diamond
1 heart	1 spade
Pass	

Opener bids a three-card heart suit over the negative response to allow room for a suit contract at the one level, and to avoid the dangerous one-notrump rebid. Responder is not much interested in the hand, but he can bid his spades cheaply; and now opener has found a haven.

OPENER	RESPONDER
♠ Q J x x	♠ A x x x
♡ K x	♡ Q x x
◇ A x x x	◇ x x
♣ Q x x	♣ J 10 x x

OPENER	RESPONDER
1 club	1 diamond
1 spade	2 spades
Pass	

Opener bids his suit at the one level, and responder raises. Game is not completely impossible, as far as the responder knows, and the raise may keep the opponents out of the auction.

OPENER	RESPONDER
♠ K J x	♠ x
♡ x x	♡ Q x x x x
◇ A Q x x	◇ K x x x
♣ K Q J x	♣ x x x

OPENER	RESPONDER
1 club	1 diamond
1 notrump	2 diamonds
Pass	

When opener rebids one notrump, showing two four-card minors, responder knows exactly where the hand should play.

OPENER	RESPONDER
♠ A K x x	♠ x
♡ K x x x	♡ A J 9 x x
◇ x x	◇ 10 x x x
♣ A J x	♣ x x x

OPENER	RESPONDER
1 club	1 diamond
1 heart	3 hearts
4 hearts	Pass

Here is one of the rare auctions that result in a game contract after the negative response. Opener bids his lower four-card major and responder shows a topnotch hand with five-card support (opener might well have only three hearts, remember) by a jump raise. Opener, having a near-maximum with top honors, goes to game.

Over a constructive response, opener's main objective is to indicate whether he has a maximum (15 to 16 points) or a minimum one-club bid; and at the same time he wants to show his suits. Here are the rules:

1. A raise of partner's suit always shows a minimum. Do not raise a major without four-card support; but since a minor-suit response promises a five-card suit, it can be raised with three cards.

2. A rebid of one notrump (over one heart or one spade) shows a minimum, while a rebid of two notrump (over two clubs or diamonds) shows a maximum.

3. A rebid in a new suit shows a maximum if it skips over a possible one-notrump rebid (for example, a two-diamond rebid over a one-heart response) but a minimum if it does not (for example, a two-spade rebid over a two-club response).

If opener's rebid shows a minimum, responder must jump or reverse (showing a "strong" hand) in order to force. But if opener's rebid shows a maximum, the auction will proceed as high as two notrump at least, and often to game.

OPENER	RESPONDER
♠ K x x	♠ Q J x x
♡ J x	♡ A Q x x
◊ A K J x	◊ x x
♣ x x x x	♣ J x x

OPENER	RESPONDER
1 club	1 heart
1 notrump	Pass

Responder bids his lower major, and opener cannot bid two diamonds (this would skip over one notrump and show a maximum) so he rebids one notrump. Responder passes, for there are not enough points to produce three notrump, and opener has denied holding either four hearts (he would raise) or four spades (opener would have bid them).

OPENER	RESPONDER
♠ A Q x x	♠ 10 x x x
♡ x x	♡ A x x
◊ Q x x x	◊ K x
♣ A K x	♣ Q x x x

OPENER	RESPONDER
1 club	1 spade
2 diamonds	2 notrump
3 spades	4 spades
Pass	

Opener cannot raise spades directly, for he has a maximum. So he shows his strength by bidding a second suit and *then* raising. Responder would have passed an immediate raise, but on this sequence he is encouraged to go on.

OPENER	RESPONDER
♠ x x	♠ K x
♡ A J x	♡ K x x
◊ K Q x x	◊ J 10 x x x
♣ K x x x	♣ Q J x

OPENER	RESPONDER
1 club	2 diamonds
3 diamonds	Pass

Responder has more than enough for his constructive two-diamond reply, but after opener shows a minimum by raising, a game contract is a poor bet.

OPENER	RESPONDER
♠ K J x x	♠ A
♡ A x	♡ J 10 x x
◊ J 10 x	◊ K Q x x x
♣ Q J x x	♣ K x x

OPENER	RESPONDER
1 club	1 heart
1 spade	3 diamonds
3 notrump	Pass

Responder prepares to show a "strong" hand by bidding his short suit first. When opener makes a minimum rebid, responder must jump to show his strength. A two-diamond rebid would be made without the spade ace, just to find the best part-score contract. However, responder would not have to jump if opener had made a maximum rebid, or if responder's first-bid (shorter) suit were *lower-ranking* than his second suit. So, with:

♠ A   ♡ J 10 x x x   ◊ K Q x x   ♣ K x x

responder would bid two diamonds over one club, and three hearts over opener's minimum two-spade or three-diamond rebid.

Over the strong response of one notrump (12 to 15 points), opener bids two of a suit—preferably his lower four-card major—to show a minimum, and bids two notrump with a maximum. If opener shows a minimum, responder can rebid two notrump with 12 points, to give opener a chance to pass if he has only 12 points also. All other rebids are forcing. If opener rebids two notrump, showing a maximum, responder can check for a 4-4 major suit fit by bidding three clubs. Any other suit response promises five-card length.

OPENER	RESPONDER
♠ A Q x x	♠ K x x
♡ K x x	♡ Q J x x x
◇ x x	◇ K x
♣ A K x x	♣ Q J x

OPENER	RESPONDER
1 club	1 notrump
2 notrump	3 hearts
4 hearts	Pass

Responder bids one notrump to show even distribution and 12 to 15 points. Opener rebids two notrump to indicate a maximum. Now when responder bids his suit, opener raises with three-card support, for if responder needed four-card support he would have bid three clubs (asking opener to bid a major), not three hearts.

When the first response is a jump to *two* notrump (16 points or more), opener shows his point-count by steps: with 12 or 13 points, three clubs; with 14 points, three diamonds; with 15 points, three hearts; with 16 points, three spades. Responder is now in a position to evaluate the slam possibilities, and if he bids three notrump that is final. Over a three-club or three-diamond reply, responder can check for a major suit fit by bidding three hearts or three spades. And over any of opener's rebids, responder may bid four clubs. This bid announces slam possibilities and initiates a search for 4-4 suit fits: Opener and responder bid their four-card suits, starting with the lower (opener bids four notrump over four clubs if his only suit is clubs) and any fit that exists will be found.

If responder jumps to two hearts or two spades over one club, opener's rebids are again artificial. Here, they show two features—whether opener has a minimum or a maximum one-club bid, and whether opener has support (as good as three to the queen or four small) for responder's suit. Opener answers by steps:

ONE STEP (two spades over two hearts, two notrump over two spades) = minimum points, poor support.

TWO STEPS (two notrump over two hearts, three clubs over two spades) = minimum points, good support.

THREE STEPS = maximum points, poor support.

FOUR STEPS = maximum points, good support.

Responder should now be able to place the contract. Since responder's jump forced to game, any rebid he makes except three notrump or three or four of his major is a slam try.

WHEN THE OPPONENTS INTERVENE

Let us suppose that you are responder, partner has opened one club, and your right-hand opponent doubles. What now? If you were going to make the negative response, pass over the double unless you are short in clubs; with fewer than three clubs, redouble, asking opener to pick another suit. If you pass the double and your left-hand opponent passes for penalties, partner will accept the contract if he has four clubs; otherwise, he asks *you* to bail out in a new suit by redoubling (with a minimum) or by bidding one diamond. If your left-hand opponent bids a suit over the double, partner will usually pass, but with a maximum he may bid a suit at the one level.

If you were going to make a constructive response, ignore the double and make your bid. However, it is no longer necessary to jump in diamonds. One diamond is constructive now, not a denial. Partner may pass any nonjump bid if he has a minimum; any rebid he makes shows a maximum. Therefore, if you have the points for a strong response, do not make a minimum takeout in a suit. When you have the requirements for one notrump, two notrump, two diamonds (now a jump response, just as in a major), two hearts, or two spades, bid it over the double. With unsuitable strong hands, pass over the double, intending to bid later or to double the opponents for penalties.

If your right-hand opponent overcalls, you pass with a negative response. You make any constructive response that you can at the one or two level, but you do not go to the three level (over a jump overcall) without a strong hand. Again, partner may pass any merely constructive response with a minimum. If you have enough for a strong response, double the overcall for penalties with at least four trumps or bid a five-card suit at the three level, jumping if necessary. With no five-card suit, bid the appropriate number of notrump if you have a stopper in the enemy suit, or cue-bid to ask partner to bid notrump if *he* has a stopper. (If he hasn't, he will bid one of his suits, preferably a major.)

OPENER		RESPONDER	
♠ A J x x		♠ K 10 x x	
♥ K x x		♥ A Q x x	
◇ x x		◇ x x	
♣ K Q x x		♣ A x x	

OPENER	OPPONENT	RESPONDER	OPPONENT
1 club	1 diamond	2 diamonds	Pass
2 spades	Pass	4 spades	Pass
Pass			

Without the interference, responder could bid one heart over one club (although one notrump would be preferable) but after the overcall one heart could (and would) be passed, and one notrump requires a stopper. So he cue-bids the opponent's suit. Opener cannot bid notrump either and bids his major instead. Now responder jumps to game (three spades over two spades would show 12 points and allow opener leeway to pass).

Next, suppose you are opener and you bid one club; partner responds, and your right-hand opponent doubles. If partner has bid the negative one diamond, you redouble with four diamonds, bid one heart or one spade if you have the suit, or pass with four clubs (you might pass with four clubs *and* a four-card major).

When it is a constructive response that has been doubled, redouble with any maximum hand. With a minimum, raise partner with four-card support, pass with three to an honor, and bid a new suit or one notrump with poorer support.

If partner responds one diamond and your opponent *over-calls*, pass with any minimum. With a maximum, you may bid a four-card spade suit at the one level (if the overcall was one heart) and you may double for takeout with two unbid four-card suits.

When the overcall comes over a constructive response, double for penalties if you have four cards in the opponent's suit. With a minimum, raise partner if you have four-card support; otherwise pass. With a maximum, bid notrump if you can stop the enemy suit; otherwise cue-bid to see if partner can.

THE STRONG TYPES OF ONE-CLUB OPENING

When you hold the very powerful sort of hand that you would open with a two-bid in standard systems, you may open one club in the Roman System. This is not absolutely neces-sary, since, as we will see, any opening one-bid in a suit is forcing; but it is best to start with one club if you have 10 or more sure tricks in your own hand, to avoid later complica-tions. When you have a little less—a hand with 8 or 9 winners and great high-card strength, with which you might stretch to open a standard two-bid—you have a choice. If you want in-formation about partner's holding in your long suits, open one club; but if you have solid suits and need general strength on the side to make a slam, tend to open in one of your suits.

1. ♠ A K 10 x x x   ♡ A Q x x x   ◇ A   ♣ x

2. ♠ A K Q J x x   ♡ A x   ◇ A J x   ♣ K x

Open one club with hand 1, but not with hand 2. It is not that you wish to force to game with one hand and not the other; it is because partner's specific holding in your suits is crucial on hand 1 but not in hand 2. Two-suiters are par-ticularly well handled by the one-club opening.

You open one club with a powerful hand, and partner makes one of the responses which we have studied: strong, construc-tive, or negative. If the response is strong or constructive, you have considerable information in advance, and you *jump* in one of your suits to give partner the good news. More often, alas, the response will be the negative one diamond. Now a rebid of two clubs or two diamonds is sufficient to indicate the strong variety of one-club bid (for you *never* go to the two level over the negative response with a 12-to-16-point balanced hand) but you must jump in a major suit. Thus any rebid over one diamond in a suit at the two level initiates the specialized responses that we present next.

Responder is compelled to show his holding in opener's

suit. He does this by steps—the bid immediately above open-er's suit (two spades over two hearts, for example) is one step and each bid higher is another step. The greater responder's support for opener's suit, the higher the bid he makes.

1 step = void or small singleton.
2 steps = two small or three small cards
3 steps = singleton ace, king, or queen
4 steps = ace, king, or queen with one or two small cards
5 steps = four small cards
6 steps = ace, king or queen with three small cards
7 steps = two of the three top honors
8 steps = two of the three top honors in a four-card suit
9 steps = ace, king, and queen

For example, on this auction:

OPENER	RESPONDER
1 club	1 heart
3 clubs	3 notrump

Responder's three-notrump reply (four steps) shows a double-ton or triplet in clubs with a high honor. Without the honor, responder would have answered one notrump (two steps) to show a doubleton or triplet. With *four*-card support and the high honor in clubs, responder would have answered four diamonds (six steps).

If opener, over this response, bids a second suit *higher-ranking than his first,* he is asking for exactly the same in-formation about his second suit.

OPENER	RESPONDER
1 club	1 diamond
2 clubs	2 hearts (two steps)
2 spades	

On this auction, responder now shows, by the same step system, his support for spades.

But if opener, over the first "step" response, bids a second suit *lower-ranking than his first,* he is asking partner for his controls in, not his support for, the second suit. Again, re-sponder gives the information by steps:

1 step = no control (no ace, king, void, or singleton)
2 steps = singleton
3 steps = void
4 steps = king
5 steps = ace

Let us see an example auction:

OPENER	RESPONDER
♠ ——	♠ Q 10 x x x
♡ A K 10 x x x x	♡ Q x
◇ A x	◇ K x x
♣ A K Q J	♣ x x x

OPENER	RESPONDER
1 club	1 spade
3 hearts	4 diamonds
5 diamonds	6 clubs
7 hearts	Pass

After the constructive response (responder is a little light in high cards, but has a five-card suit to compensate) opener must jump (a bid of only *two* hearts here would show a maximum *weak* one-club bid). Responder makes a four-step answer, showing a guarded high honor. Opener next bids diamonds, a lower-ranking suit in which he wants to learn responder's controls. The answer of six clubs once again is four steps, showing the king of diamonds. That is all opener needs to bid the grand slam. Simple!

If opener wants information about *support* in two suits, he must take care to bid his *lower*-ranking suit first, regardless of his distribution. Responder will not be deceived—opener is the captain, and will place the final contract.

OPENER	RESPONDER
♠ A K Q 10 x x	♠ x
♡ A	♡ K J x x x x
◇ A	◇ K J x x x
♣ K Q J x x	♣ x

OPENER	RESPONDER
1 club	1 heart
3 clubs	3 diamonds
3 spades	3 notrump
4 spades	Pass

Over the constructive response, opener jumps in his lower suit so that he can find out about responder's support for both spades and clubs. When responder shows a singleton or void in clubs by the one-step reply, opener checks on spades. Responder denies support for that suit too, so opener signs off at game in his better suit.

POWERFUL BALANCED HANDS

When you hold the third type of one-club opening, the 4-3-3-3 or 4-4-3-2 hand with 21 to 26 points—a standard two-notrump or three-notrump opening bid (except that you are not required to have stoppers in all suits; you might even have a small doubleton in one)—you jump in notrump over partner's negative or constructive response to one club. If partner has bid one heart or one spade, jump to two notrump; if he has bid two clubs or two diamonds, jump to three notrump. With any of these hands:

1. ♠ A Q x   ♡ K J x   ◇ A K J x   ♣ K x x
2. ♠ A Q J x   ♡ A Q J x   ◇ A K Q   ♣ x x
3. ♠ A K   ♡ A K Q x   ◇ K J 10 x   ♣ A Q x

open one club and jump to two notrump over one heart or one spade, to three notrump over two clubs or two diamonds. These rebids are, of course, forcing; slam is very likely after a constructive response.

If partner has, instead, responded one diamond, there may not be even a game in the hand. You rebid *three* notrump with a maximum (24 to 26 points, as in hand 3 above) and two notrump with a minimum (21 to 23 points, as in hands 1 and 2). After your jump to two notrump, partner should sign off with 0 to 3 points. He will pass if he is balanced and he will bid three diamonds, three hearts or three spades if he is unbalanced. (You may raise to four of a major with a maximum and strong support.)

When partner has the upper-level one-diamond response (4 to 8 points), he can raise to three notrump or bid a game in a suit. These bids are final. Last, he can probe for a 4-4 major suit fit by bidding three clubs over your two-notrump rebid. You answer three diamonds with no four-card major, three hearts or three spades with that suit, or three notrump with both majors. After three notrump, partner will bid four in the suit just under his four-card major, allowing the strong hand to declarer:

OPENER   RESPONDER
♠ K Q 10 x   ♠ x x
♡ A K J x   ♡ Q x x x
◇ J x   ◇ x x x
♣ A K J   ♣ Q x x x

OPENER	RESPONDER
1 club	1 diamond
2 notrump	3 clubs
3 notrump	4 diamonds
4 hearts	Pass

If you have a maximum, and jump to three notrump over the one-diamond response, partner can close the auction with a game bid if he is unbalanced, or pass if he is balanced. A four-club bid checks for majors: You answer four diamonds with neither major, four hearts with hearts or both (partner can now try four spades), four spades with spades only. Should no fit be found, partner signs off with four notrump. Last, partner may try for slam with 7 or 8 points by raising to four notrump directly. This asks you to initiate a search for a suit fit by bidding your lower-ranking four-card suit at the five level. You and partner will bid your suits "up the line" and any 4-4 fit will be found.

When you jump in notrump over a constructive response, partner can raise notrump to show a flat, bare minimum—8 to 9 points. More often, he will move towards slam by bidding a suit, either a rebid of his original suit or a new one. If he makes any suit-bid you are expected to answer by steps, whether you have a maximum or minimum point-count and whether you have good or poor support for the suit he asks in. One step = minimum, poor support; two steps = minimum, good support; three steps = maximum, poor support; four steps = maximum, good support. And any further new-suit bid by responder over your reply asks again in *that* suit:

OPENER	RESPONDER
♠ A x	♠ K Q x x x
♡ K Q x	♡ A x x
◇ A K Q x	◇ x x
♣ A K x x	♣ x x x

OPENER	RESPONDER
1 club	1 spade
2 notrump	3 spades
4 diamonds	6 notrump
Pass	

After opener's jump in notrump, responder asks in spades. The three-step answer—a maximum with poor support—tells responder all he wants to know. There are enough points for slam, and the slam must not play in spades.

DEFENSE AGAINST THE ONE-CLUB OPENING

When your opponents are playing the Roman Club System, their one-club opening bid should make the auction rather easy for you. The opening bid has already told you a great deal about opener's strength and distribution, and the response will fill in the rest of the picture for you. All you have to do is listen, and the opponents will tell you whether it is safe to bid.

Therefore, your normal tendency should be to pass over the one-club opening and get a little more information before you enter the auction. On all the hands in which your side has more points than the opponents have, the bidding will still be at the one level when your turn comes again; it will be practically as convenient to bid at the later stage, and a great deal safer. So why put your neck on the block by bidding directly?

Why? Well, one good reason is distribution. When you are unbalanced, you can compete effectively even if the opponents have more than half the deck, and the hand may belong to you if partner has a good fit. So there is no point in waiting to hear the response; if you knew in advance it would be constructive, you still would want to bid.

You should pass *any* balanced hand over one club, no matter how strong. If the response is the negative one diamond, opener will rebid at the one level—most often one heart, occasionally one spade, rarely one notrump. Now double with an opening bid or more. This is a takeout double, but if partner has the right hand he may be able to convert it into a penalty double to good effect. In any event, it is much better to bid now that both opponents are limited; on the first round, you might have walked into a powerful hand on your left or even into a 26-point hand on your right. And you have no suit to run to in an emergency. With:

♠ A Q x ♡ K J x ◇ A J x x ♣ Q x x

pass over a one-club opening. If the response is one diamond and opener rebids one heart, double. Partner should treat this as a normal takeout double of a one-bid and should jump with about 10 points as usual. But he can pass the double with a fair four-card heart holding and scattered values, counting on you to have a balanced hand. If he responds one spade, you will make a mild game try of one notrump.

With the example hand above, you will stay out of the auction if the response is constructive. *You* have a lot of points, but the opponents have more; partner has scarcely a face card.

Overcalls should be used freely on unbalanced hands. Any respectable five-card suit should be bid if you have a singleton on the side. Overcalls should have a wide range of strength; overcall one spade with:

1. ♠ K Q 10 x x   ♡ x   ◇ Q J x x   ♣ x x x
2. ♠ K J 10 x x x   ♡ x   ◇ J 10 x x   ♣ A x
3. ♠ A K J x x   ♡ x x   ◇ A J x x   ♣ x x

However, the hand should not be much stronger than hand 3. Use the jump overcall to show better unbalanced hands, with excellent game prospects opposite a scattering of cards in partner's hand. Bid two hearts over one club with:

♠ x x   ♡ A K Q x x x   ◇ K Q 10 x   ♣ x
♠ x   ♡ K Q J x x   ◇ A J 10 x x   ♣ A x

For freakish distributions, use the double-jump overcall. This may well freeze the opponents out of a 4-4 major-suit fit, for responder cannot bid at the three level without 12 points at least. Bid three diamonds over one club with:

♠ x x x   ♡ x   ◇ K Q 10 9 x x x   ♣ K x
♠ x x x   ♡ A x x   ◇ Q J 10 9 x x x   ♣ ——

Any overcall in clubs—single, jump, or double jump—is natural, showing club length.

The double of one club should be used to show strong distributional support for both major suits. The least you should have is four of each, and then your pattern should be 4-4-4-1. The longer your major suits, the less you need to double:

♠ A K x x   ♡ K J x x   ◇ x   ♣ Q 10 x x
♠ K Q x x x   ♡ A J x x   ◇ x x x   ♣ x
♠ Q J 10 x x   ♡ A J 10 x x   ◇ x   ♣ x x

These are all minimum doubles of one club. Partner should bid (or jump in) a major suit if he has one. He may even reply in a three-card suit if he has a strong preference for one major over the other. With no preference, he bids one diamond and lets you take your pick.

The one-notrump overcall directly over one club is useless to show strength—you pass any balanced hand. So it should be used for minors as the double is for majors (but have at least 5-5). If, unluckily, you are dealt one long major suit and one long minor, overcall.

When one club is opened on your left, you hear the response before you have to bid, so your problems are different. If the response is constructive, pass any balanced hand. But you may make a "normal" pattern takeout double of responder's suit, promising support for the unbid suits with emphasis on unbid majors. Almost always, you should have a singleton or void in responder's suit for this action. Overcall with any freakish pattern, but stay out of the auction with 5-3-3-2 hands, however strong, unless you have a solid suit.

If the response is one diamond, double with balanced hands of 14 points or more. Partner may well be able to double any run-out. The opponents could conceivably have only 12 points between them. Even when you run into the 21- to 26-point hand behind you, you are unlikely to be penalized. Opener must jump to two notrump; his redouble here has a conventional meaning.

Double one diamond also with an unbalanced major-suit hand. Remember, opener will redouble when he has four diamonds, so the chance that your double will be passed out is slight. And if opener runs to a major, partner will pass it around for you to double for penalties. But if partner doubles an eventual minor-suit or one-notrump contract, take out.

Overcall, jump-overcall and double-jump over one diamond just as you would directly over one club. And use the one-notrump overcall as unusual for minors. With only one long minor, bid it. Overcalls in clubs or diamonds are natural, for the opponents' bids are artificial.

II. The One-Notrump Opening Bid

There is a gap between the weak one-club opening for balanced hands of 12 to 16 points and the strong one-club opening for balanced hands of 21 to 26 points. With 17 to 20 points and no five-card suit * or singleton, open one notrump.

---

* Although the Roman System tolerates (but just barely) a one-notrump opening bid with a hand that contains a five-card suit, there is no record of a Roman player in World Championship competition opening one notrump with any distribution except 4-3-3-3 or 4-4-3-2.

1. ♠ A Q x   ♡ K J x   ◊ K 10 x x   ♣ A K x

2. ♠ A K J x   ♡ A Q J x   ◊ x x   ♣ Q x x

3. ♠ A Q   ♡ K 10 x   ◊ A Q x x x   ♣ Q x x

Hands 1 and 2 are one-notrump opening bids, but hand 3 is not. In the Roman System, hand pattern and point value, not location of honors, determines the opening bid.

As responder, you have three types of action over the one-notrump opening: negative, invitational, and strong. There are two negative responses. Pass, of course, is one; pass with 0 to 5 points and a balanced hand. The other negative response is two clubs, used when you want to sign off in a suit. Opener is compelled to rebid two diamonds, and you now pass with diamonds or sign off at two hearts, two spades, or three clubs. Opener will normally pass any rebid after two clubs, but he may raise two hearts or two spades with 20 points and at least three-card support including two of the three top honors.

OPENER	RESPONDER
♠ A K x x	♠ x x
♡ K Q x	♡ J x x x x x
◊ K J x	◊ x x x
♣ A x x	♣ x x

OPENER	RESPONDER
1 notrump	2 clubs
2 diamonds	2 hearts
3 hearts	Pass

Preparing to sign off in hearts, responder uses the negative two-club bid. Opener's two-diamond rebid is forced; but when responder follows through with two hearts, opener tries again. However, responder is not interested in game. (With a queen on the side he would accept the invitation.)

Responder's invitational responses to one notrump are two notrump, three hearts, and three spades. The raise to two notrump shows 6 to 7 points and balanced distribution. Opener will pass with a minimum or go on with a maximum. Should he decide to rebid over two notrump, he can bid three notrump directly, or stop off on the way to check for a major-suit fit, by bidding three clubs. This asks responder to bid three notrump if he has no four-card major, or to bid the suit under his major if he has one. Thus, responder answers three diamonds to show hearts (if opener is really interested in spades, he will

now bid three spades over three diamonds, for responder may
have four of *each* major) and three hearts to show spades and
deny hearts. This is designed, of course, to prevent opener's
very strong hand from coming down as dummy; it should be
concealed and led up to.

OPENER	RESPONDER
♠ A Q x x	♠ K x x x
♡ K x	♡ Q x x x
◊ A K x x	◊ x x
♣ K x x	♣ J x x

OPENER	RESPONDER
1 notrump	2 notrump
3 clubs	3 diamonds
3 spades	4 spades
Pass	

Responder scrapes up a raise to two notrump, and opener
checks for a 4-4 fit in spades. Responder "bids" his hearts by
responding three diamonds, opener now bids his suit, and
the fit is found, and the reasonable, although "thin," game
contract is reached.

The invitational responses of three hearts and three spades
over a one-notrump opening show specific hands: a six-card
major suit no better than A-J high and no poorer than K-J,
with no outside values. Over this jump, opener places the
contract: He may pass, raise, or bid three notrump, according
to his hand—he should know exactly what can be made.

OPENER	RESPONDER
♠ A x x	♠ x x x
♡ K Q x	♡ A 10 x x x x
◊ A x x x	◊ x x x
♣ A x x	♣ x

OPENER	RESPONDER
1 notrump	3 hearts
3 notrump	Pass

Opener has a minimum notrump, but he can count nine tricks.

All other responses to one notrump are strong and forcing
to game. Jumps to three notrump, four hearts and four spades
are the normal closing bids; responder wants to play right
there. Two diamonds over one notrump is "Stayman." Opener
bids a major suit if he has one and two notrump if he hasn't.

Suit takeouts—two hearts, two spades, three clubs,* three diamonds *—promise five-card or longer suits and ask opener to show, by steps, the quality of his hand and of his support. Again,

> 1 step = minimum opening, minimum support
> 2 steps = minimum opening, good support (Q-x-x, x-x-x-x, or better)
> 3 steps = maximum opening, minimum support
> 4 steps = maximum opening, good support

If responder now bids game in his suit or in notrump, that is final. But he may, instead, bid a new suit and ask opener about his support for the second suit. Since opener has already indicated his strength, he answers only "poor support" (one step) or "good support" (two steps). Let us see an example:

OPENER	RESPONDER
♠ x x x	♠ A K x x x
♡ A x	♡ Q 10 x x x
◇ K Q J x	◇ x
♣ A K Q x	♣ x x

OPENER	RESPONDER
1 notrump	2 spades
3 diamonds	3 hearts
3 spades	3 notrump
Pass	

Responder's two-spade takeout initiates the reply by steps; opener skips over no trump and clubs, making a three-step answer—maximum points but poor fit. Responder now tries hearts, but opener's one-step answer says "no fit here either." So responder bids the safer notrump game, knowing that opener's strength must be heavily concentrated in the minors.

Last, responder can show his exact point-count to opener, asking partner to evaluate the slam or grand slam potential. He does this in a stepped series starting with four clubs (opener one notrump—responder four clubs), which shows 14 points. Four diamonds shows 15 points. The series skips over four hearts and four spades, which are natural, and resumes with

---

* Responder should be quite unbalanced or very strong to use these jump minor-suit takeouts. His normal course with a minor suit is to jump to three notrump.

four notrump for 16 points. It goes all the way up to five notrump, which shows 21 points. Opener can sign off with a minimum notrump bid, bid six notrump or seven notrump, or bid his lower-ranking four-card suit to inaugurate a search for a 4-4 fit:

OPENER	RESPONDER
♠ Q x x	♠ K x x
♡ K x	♡ A Q x
◇ A K 10 x	◇ Q J x x
♣ K Q x x	♣ A x x

OPENER	RESPONDER
1 notrump	4 notrump
5 clubs	5 diamonds
6 diamonds	Pass

The four notrump response shows 16 points, so opener can count the points required for slam; however, there is nothing to spare, and a suit may be safer. (Responder did not bid six notrump for the same reason, and also to take care of the possibility that partner had "cheated" and opened a good-looking 16 points.) So opener initiates the search for a suit by bidding his lower-ranking four-carder; responder follows through by bidding *his,* and the superior six-diamond slam is reached.

On defense against the Roman opening bid of one notrump, stay out of the auction—except to double artificial bids for leads.

III. One-Diamond, One-Heart and One-Spade Opening Bids

Opening bids of one diamond, one heart and one spade are forcing in the Roman System. They have an enormous range of strength, going from a 12-point skinny minimum up to hands that would be opened with two notrump, or with shaded two-bids, in standard systems. But they are limited in distribution—every one-diamond, one-heart or one-spade opening bid contains at least one suit of five cards or more (not necessarily, in fact not usually, the suit that is opened). All balanced patterns are opened one club or one notrump, and there are specialized bids for three-suited hands, as we will see in the next chapter. So these opening bids are made only with one-suited and two-suited unbalanced distribution.

"Canapé"* style—bidding short suits ahead of long ones—is used rigorously; if opener has two suits he almost always bids the shorter first, regardless of his strength. Opener's *second* suit, then, is the five-card or longer suit that justified his opening bid; his first suit is commonly of four-card, and occasionally of three-card, length. There is no concept of a reverse by opener in the ordinary American sense: a one-heart opening followed by a two-spade rebid shows five spades, not necessarily a strong hand.

The general development of auctions that start with a one-diamond, one-heart or one-spade opening is this: Opener shows his distribution and limits his strength with his first two bids; responder indicates his strength immediately, then limits it further, showing distributional features also, with his rebid. By the third round of bidding, the hand will be either passed out at a part-score or bid to a game, unless slam tries have been initiated. Let us see how it works.

THE OPENING BID

Opener will have either a two-suited hand or a hand with only one long suit. With the two-suiter, he has no problem choosing his opening bid; he bids the shorter suit. (However, holding a strong five- or six-card major suit and a minimum hand in high cards, opener may bid and rebid his long suit, even with a side four-card suit, in order to limit his hand. With two equally long suits, he opens in the lower-ranking suit.

♠ K x x x	♡ x x	◇ A K J x x x	♣ x	One spade
♠ A x	♡ K Q J 10 x	◇ Q J x x	♣ K x	One diamond
♠ K Q x x x	♡ K Q x x x	◇ A x	♣ A	One heart

It is with the one-suiter, oddly enough, that opener may have a choice of bids. This is because he will have to rebid his suit at his second turn—he has no convenient side five-card suit to bid next. A minimum rebid of his suit will show 12 to 14 points, while a jump rebid will show a semi-solid suit, six cards or longer, with 15 to 17 high-card points. Hands like:

| ♠ A J x x x | ♡ K x | ◇ A Q x | ♣ Q x x |
| ♠ K Q x | ♡ A Q 10 x x | ◇ K x x | ♣ K x |

---

* Developed by France's great player Pierre Albarran.

fit into neither category of rebid. So opener bids a three-card suit and shows his five-card suit by bidding it on the second round. This does not *promise* extra values, but at least it does not deny them. Obviously, opener prefers to bid a false suit *lower* in rank than his true suit, so both example hands are opened one diamond.

A different sort of dilemma occurs when opener has a one-suiter in clubs. He cannot open one club when he has a five-card or longer suit. The solution is the same: Bid a three-card suit first and rebid in clubs. With:

1. ♠ K x x   ♡ A Q   ◇ Q x x   ♣ Q J x x x
2. ♠ x   ♡ A x x   ◇ K x x   ♣ K Q 10 x x x
3. ♠ x   ♡ Q x x   ◇ A x   ♣ A K Q 10 x x x

you may not open one club. With hands 1 and 2, open one diamond, preferring to "lie" about a minor suit (only your opening bid is a lie; your rebid, in clubs, will be quite honest) rather than about a major. Open one heart with hand 3. Try never to bid a doubleton, although with 7-2-2-2 distribution you will have to. Two-suiters, with clubs as the shorter suit, are no problem, as we will see in the next chapter; they are opened with two-bids, not one diamond, one heart or one spade.

RESPONSES

Responder may not pass the opening bid. His responses fall into three categories, just as over one club: negative, constructive, and strong. The constructive responses start at a slightly higher level than they do over one club; 9 points is the minimum, and 9-point—or even occasional 10-point—hands may be better handled with a negative response first and a strong rebid afterward.

There are two negative responses: the raise of opener's suit, and the bid one step higher than the opening (one heart over one diamond; one spade over one heart; one notrump over one spade). The difference between the two negative responses is simply that the raise contains good support (four and often five cards) in opener's suit, and the step response does not. (With 4-3-3-3 distribution and fewer than 4 points, do not raise. Make the step response.) Holding:

♠ x x   ♡ A Q x   ◇ J x x x x   ♣ J x x

respond two diamonds to a one-diamond opening; one spade to a one-heart opening; one notrump to a one-spade opening.

With:

♠xxx   ♥Jxxx   ♦xxx   ♣Jxx

respond one heart to one diamond; one spade to one heart; one notrump to one spade. You may not pass, and it is inadvisable to raise.

The constructive responses are suit-bids at a minimum level, and the jump in the artificial negative suit (one heart—two spades). This jump, which gets the auction up rather high, requires special values: 10 to 12 points, a five-card suit at least, and two of the three top honors. The other suit-bids require 9 or usually 10 points at least, but do not promise any suit quality or length. In choosing the suit in which to make a constructive response, these are the principles to follow:

1. With a balanced hand: Bid a suit at the one level (over one diamond) if you can. Bid a minor suit (even a three-card suit) at the two level, intending to bid notrump or to raise partner's rebid next. With minimum count, give thought to making a negative response instead; you should have 10 points to go to the two level.

2. With one long suit: With 9 to 11 points, bid your suit and then rebid it. With 12 or more points and a suit in which you do not care to jump on the next round, bid a false suit first (lower-ranking if possible) and bid your long suit next.

3. With a 5-4 two-suiter: Bid your four-card suit first and your five-card suit next; but if your five-card suit is the higher-ranking, and you have 9 to 11 points, bid the five-card suit first and rebid it (you may not reverse with fewer than 12 points). With 12 points or more, jump in your five-card suit at your second turn if bidding it at a minimum level would not constitute a reverse. (But do not get above three notrump; if opener has bid the other suits, bid three notrump instead.)

4. With a 5-5 two-suiter: With 9 to 11 points, bid the higher, then the lower; with 12 or more, reverse.

The strong responses are one notrump (except over one spade), a jump raise, and a jump in a new suit (except the "negative" suit). The one-notrump response is like a normal jump to *two* notrump—a balanced hand (possibly with a weak five-card suit), stoppers in all unbid suits, 12 to 15 points.

The two-notrump response has the same distribution, but is stronger still—16 to 18 points, like the normal jump to three notrump. The jump raise of opener's suit shows 10 to 14 points and at least five trumps including two of the three top honors. Without the top honors, but with the other requirements, responder jumps to four in opener's major suit. The jump shift is an immediate slam try, an asking bid. It will be treated under Slam Bidding.

THE AUCTION AFTER A NEGATIVE RESPONSE

When responder has raised the suit opened, opener has a choice of actions. With any 12- to 14-point hand, he passes—game is out of the question, so there is no point in showing his second suit if he has 5-4 or 5-3 distribution. Responder has at least four trumps, so the contract should be playable. Open one heart and pass a two-heart response with:

  ♠ Q 10 x x x   ♡ A K x x   ◇ K x x   ♣ x

  ♠ K x x   ♡ A Q x x x   ◇ K x x   ♣ Q x

  ♠ J x x   ♡ Q x x   ◇ A K   ♣ K J x x x

Note that opener does not run out of hearts in the third example. With a minimum opening, pass and take your chances in a 4-3 fit. (Responder may well have five hearts.)

With a 15- to 17-point hand, opener may try for game. If he bids a new suit, that is his long one, and responder is allowed to pass. (Responder, with a minimum, tends to pass rather than return to the first suit, when opener's second suit is higher-ranking than his first or when the second suit is clubs; the first suit is likely to be false.) Responder has these options: to pass, or to give a preference back to the first suit, with minimum strength; to raise opener's second suit, jump in opener's second suit, jump in opener's first suit, or bid notrump, with maximum values or fitting cards. Here are a few examples:

OPENER	RESPONDER
♠ A Q x x x	♠ K x x
♡ K x	♡ Q x x
◇ A J x x	◇ Q 10 x x x
♣ K x	♣ x x

OPENER	RESPONDER
1 diamond	2 diamonds
2 spades	3 spades
4 spades	Pass

Opener is strong enough to try for game by bidding his long suit over the negative response. Responder has good fitting cards (although he discounts his heart queen) and so can raise the spades, knowing that partner has five at least. Opener, with a maximum, goes on. Without the queen of spades he would have passed. If responder had held the queen of spades instead of the queen of hearts, he would have jumped to four spades over two spades.

OPENER	RESPONDER
♠ K Q J x x	♠ x x x
♡ A x x	♡ J 10 x x
◊ K x	◊ A x x x
♣ K 10 x	♣ x x

OPENER	RESPONDER
1 heart	2 hearts
2 spades	Pass

Opener starts with a false heart bid, to give himself a satisfactory rebid. When partner raises, he shows his spades. Responder passes, realizing that the hand is playable in spades and that opener is likely to have only three hearts. With five hearts and one or two spades he would have gone back to hearts. With five hearts and greater strength, he could jump to four hearts.

Opener can try for game over a major-suit raise by reraising to three. This asks responder to go to game with 7 or 8 points, or more. Normally, this invitation is made with 5-4-2-2 hands (four in the bid suit, of course) when responder's holding in opener's longer suit is not crucial: Open one spade, and bid three spades over a raise to two spades, with:

♠ A Q 10 x   ♡ K x   ◊ K Q J x x   ♣ x x

Opener can jump to game in a major that has been raised if he has 18 points or more, usually in a hand that has strong distributional features. Open one heart and jump to four hearts after a raise with:

♠ A J x   ♡ K Q x x   ◊ A K J x x   ♣ x

Opener's jump to three notrump over the raise shows a *very* powerful—a 21- to 24-point—5-3-3-2 hand which was not opened one club because it had a five-card suit. Opener's *jump* in a new suit is an asking bid, a slam try made with an uncommonly unbalanced hand. (See the chapter on Slam Bidding.)

When responder has made the negative step response, the more common minimum reply, opener may not pass. With the minimum one-suited hand (12 to 14 points) he rebids his suit. He may jump in his suit with a solid or semisolid six-card or longer suit and 15 to 17 points in high cards, just as in standard bidding. With hands that lack a strong suit and are in between the two rebids, or are stronger still, he would have opened in a false suit.

Responder will normally pass the minimum rebid (but may take out in a very long suit of his own, having limited his hand already). Over the jump rebid, responder raises or bids three notrump with 6 or 7 (or more) points. He usually passes with fewer points than this.

If opener has a two-suited pattern (or has made a false bid initially) he now bids his long suit. When, as frequently happens, the negative step response is made in opener's long suit, rebids can be very accurate. Opener's rebid of one notrump in these sequences:

OPENER	RESPONDER	OPENER	RESPONDER
1 diamond	1 heart	1 heart	1 spade
1 notrump		1 notrump	

indicates that he has five or more cards in the "negative" suit (hearts in the first example, spades in the second) and the minimum of 12 to 14 points. With 15 to 17 points, he bids two in his long major; and with 18 to 21 points he jumps to three. When his long suit is not the one in which the negative response has been made, opener bids it at a minimum level with any strength hand in the two lower ranges—12 to 17 points. Holding the 18- to 21-point range, he jumps in his suit.

Over the one-notrump rebid, responder will sign off (there is unlikely to be a game with 12 to 14 points opposite a negative response). He may bid two of the negative suit; or two of opener's first suit (but only with a marked preference) ; or, with no fit, a long suit of his own; or he may pass.

OPENER	RESPONDER
♠ K Q 10 x x	♠ J x
♡ Q x x x	♡ x x x
◇ A x x	◇ K Q x
♣ x	♣ Q 10 x x x

OPENER	RESPONDER
1 heart	1 spade
1 notrump	2 spades
Pass	

Opener shows a "canapé" with a five-card or longer spade suit by rebidding one notrump. Note that responder gives his preference in opener's long suit. Opener's hearts are probably of four-card and possibly of three-card length. Even with his close-to-maximum negative, responder does not look for game over one notrump. But had opener rebid two spades instead, responder would have tried two notrump. And over a three-spade rebid, responder has more than enough to bid game.

When opener bids a new suit over the negative response, responder should make an effort to keep the auction going if he has a maximum. He may raise the second suit, or bid notrump, or—with no fit—bid a new suit of his own. But he should pass any 0- to 7-point hand unless it has strong distributional support or a wealth of key cards. When opener *jumps* in a new suit, responder should look for game if he has any feature that will provide a trick. If responder has a maximum for a negative response, with a good fitting hand, even a slam try may be in view.

If opener bids two notrump over the step response, he shows the 5-3-3-2 hand with 21 to 24 points—a normal two notrump opening with five cards in the suit he opened.

AUCTION AFTER CONSTRUCTIVE RESPONSES

Generally, auctions that bring forth a constructive response proceed to game. Only when a minimum constructive response faces a minimum opening bid will the partnership stop short; extra value in either hand usually results in game.

Opener's rebids are much like those over the negative step response. With a one-suiter, a long, strong suit, with 15 to 17 points, he jumps; and in this situation the jump rebid is game-forcing. He makes the minimum rebid of his suit with 12 to 14 points. Responder, holding a minimum himself, will pass, or rebid his suit, or bid a second suit without reversing, or bid two notrump; all of these rebids are most likely to be passed by opener. When responder has the extra value needed for game, he must jump to game in opener's suit, jump in his first or a new suit, reverse into a new suit, or jump to three notrump. The raise of opener's suit is invitational, but not forcing.

In all cases in which responder's rebid is in a new suit, this second suit is his long one; his first suit may be as long, but is probably shorter, and when responder has forced with his rebid the first suit may be wholly false. (See responder's choice of constructive responses, page 109.)

OPENER	RESPONDER
♠ J x	♠ K x x x
♡ A K J x x	♡ x x
◇ A x x	◇ K x x
♣ x x x	♣ K Q x x

OPENER	RESPONDER
1 heart	2 clubs
2 hearts	Pass

Observe the two-club response. Responder cannot bid one spade, for this would be the negative step. But there is no danger of missing a 4-4 spade fit. *Opener cannot have four spades and open one heart.* And if opener has five spades, he will bid two spades over two clubs. Over the actual two-heart rebid, responder can safely pass. Opener has no more than 14 points, so a game will not be missed. With three hearts and two diamonds:

♠ K x x x   ♡ x x x   ◇ K x   ♣ K Q x x

responder would invite by bidding three hearts over two hearts. With a singleton heart:

♠ K x x x   ♡ x   ◇ K x x x   ♣ K Q x x

responder would sign off with two notrump over two hearts.

OPENER	RESPONDER
♠ x x	♠ A Q J x x x
♡ K x x	♡ Q x x
◇ A Q x x x	◇ x x
♣ A J x	♣ x x

OPENER	RESPONDER
1 diamond	1 spade
2 diamonds	2 spades
Pass	

Opener shows his minimum (here, the topnotch minimum) one-suiter and responder signs off by rebidding his suit. Opener is close to making a game try; even with this hand he might hazard two notrump, and he surely would with so much as a tenspot extra. If one of his honors were in spades, he would raise.

OPENER	RESPONDER
♠ K J x x x x	♠ x
♡ A x x	♡ Q 10 x x x x
◇ K x	◇ A x x
♣ J x	♣ A Q x

OPENER	RESPONDER
1 spade	2 clubs
2 spades	3 hearts
4 hearts	Pass

Responder is loath to jump-rebid in his broken heart suit, so he prepares a forcing rebid by bidding a false lower-ranking suit first. Opener makes his minimum rebid and responder reverses into his long suit, which opener is happy to raise.

If opener bids a new suit (his long suit) over the constructive response, his range is from 12 to 17 points. Therefore responder may not pass. Responder's rebids are much the same as over the rebid of opener's suit. With 9 to 11 points, responder rebids his first suit, bids a new (long) lower-ranking suit, bids two notrump (but not three notrump, if opener has gone to the three level), raises opener's second suit, or, with four-card support, goes back to opener's first suit. All these responses may—and likely will—be passed if opener also has a minimum. So, with 12 points or more, responder must jump-rebid his first suit, reverse into a new (long) suit, jump in a new (long) lower-ranking suit, bid three notrump, jump or bid game in opener's second suit, or give a jump preference with four in opener's first suit. All these responses are forcing to game. Notice that responder will be in trouble if he has bid two diamonds over a one-heart opening, for example with:

♠ A J x   ♡ K x x   ◇ Q x x x x   ♣ x x

If opener now rebids three clubs, responder has no reasonable action. Three diamonds is unthinkable with such a suit; three hearts may result in a 3-3 trump "fit"; three notrump could put the partnership into a 22-point game contract. This is the sort of 10-point hand with which a negative first response of one spade is more prudent. Responder can compensate with his rebid: If opener bids one notrump over one

spade, responder will jump to three spades. Responder will
bid two notrump over two clubs, and three diamonds over two
diamonds; and responder will raise a minimum two-heart rebid
by opener. In general, responder should be conservative in
making constructive replies, preferring the negative response
in doubtful cases, with the intention of making an aggressive
second bid.

OPENER	RESPONDER
♠ K Q x	♠ J x x
♡ J x x	♡ A x x
◇ x	◇ K Q 10 9 x x
♣ A Q x x x x	♣ x

OPENER	RESPONDER
1 heart	2 diamonds
3 clubs	3 diamonds
Pass	

Opener cannot start with one club, so he bids his lower
three-card holding instead; he avoids opening a three-card
spade suit whenever possible. Responder can answer two diamonds because his fine suit will provide a rebid. Opener shows
his long suit, and responder signs off. Now opener passes, for
he has a minimum facing a minimum; with the upper range of
his "canapé" rebid, 15 to 17 points, he would try three
notrump.

OPENER	RESPONDER
♠ x x	♠ K J 10 x
♡ K Q 10 x x	♡ J x x
◇ A K x x	◇ x x
♣ A x	♣ K J x x

OPENER	RESPONDER
1 diamond	1 spade
2 hearts	3 hearts
4 hearts	Pass

Responder has a skinny constructive response, but has the
requirements since he can bid at the one level. Over opener's
rebid in a new suit, responder shows his minimum by raising
(he knows that opener has at least five hearts, remember).
Opener goes to game, since he has an upper-level hand. With
the 12- to 14-point "canapé" (lacking the king of diamonds,

for example), he would pass. If responder had an extra ace or
king, he would jump to four hearts over two hearts.

OPENER	RESPONDER
♠ x x	♠ J 10 x
♡ K Q x x	♡ A J x x
◊ A K J x x	◊ Q x x
♣ x x	♣ A J x

OPENER	RESPONDER
1 heart	2 clubs
2 diamonds	3 hearts
4 hearts	Pass

Responder does not have the specific trump requirements for
the jump raise, and avoids the strong one-notrump response
because of his doubtful spade holding and his good heart support; he bids a three-card minor. Over opener's two-diamond
rebid, responder gives a *jump* preference; two hearts would
show a minimum hand. Opener bids game, confident of four-
card support (he would pass *two* hearts). If opener had,
instead, the strong one-suiter:

♠ A x x   ♡ K Q x   ◊ A K J x x   ♣ x x

he could bid three notrump over three hearts. Without value in
spades, he would rebid a six-card diamond suit, show club
support, or gamble out a 4-3 fit for a heart game.

OPENER	RESPONDER
♠ A K x x	♠ Q x
♡ K x	♡ A Q x x
◊ x x	◊ A Q x x x
♣ K J x x x	♣ x x

OPENER	RESPONDER
1 spade	2 hearts
3 clubs	3 notrump
Pass	

Responder prepares to show his suits in the normal Roman
order—shorter first—in case the auction should take a slam-
mish turn. But over opener's three-club rebid, responder may
not bid three diamonds. This would show a minimum 5-4, as
it is not a reverse; and opener would pass. Responder is unwilling to go above the most likely game contract by jumping

to four diamonds; so he bids three notrump. Opener can be pretty sure that responder has long diamonds for this auction: With long hearts, responder would have reversed into them by bidding diamonds first; with balanced distribution, responder would have ignored the four-card major and bid a three-card minor instead.

With certain two-suiters, opener has a different rebid available over the constructive response—a notrump bid at the cheapest level. These sequences:

1.		**2.**	
OPENER	RESPONDER	OPENER	RESPONDER
1 heart	2 clubs	1 diamond	1 spade
2 notrump		1 notrump	

3.	
OPENER	RESPONDER
1 spade	2 hearts
2 notrump	

mean that opener has an unbid five-card minor suit (diamonds in the first example, clubs in the second, clubs or diamonds in the third); the upper range of strength—15 to 17 points, and a hand that is satisfactory for notrump play; and 5-4-2-2 distribution with a stopper in the fourth suit.

Open one heart, and rebid two notrump over two diamonds, holding:

    ♠ K x   ♡ A Q x x   ♢ J x   ♣ A Q 10 x x

But make the normal "canapé" rebid of three clubs with minimum strength, or with more unbalanced distribution, or lacking a spade stopper.

OPENER	RESPONDER
♠ A K x x	♠ Q x
♡ A Q	♡ x
♢ x x	♢ K J 10 x x x
♣ Q 10 9 x x	♣ K J x x

OPENER	RESPONDER
1 spade	2 diamonds
2 notrump	3 clubs
3 notrump	Pass

Note that responder bids his long suit first, since he is not strong enough to reverse. He intends to rebid diamonds, but when opener bids two notrump, responder supports opener's club suit, suggesting a hole in hearts and probing for a minor-suit game. Opener has enough heart stoppers to prefer no-trump. The advantage of the specialized notrump rebid is apparent in this example. Had opener rebid three clubs instead, responder would have raised and the superior notrump contract would have been by-passed.

When opener raises the constructive suit response directly in this one sequence:

OPENER	RESPONDER
1 diamond	1 spade
2 spades	

he shows a canapé with spades his five-card suit. All other constructive responses are made at the two level, and opener's raise to three normally indicates a one-suited minimum (5-3-3-2 distribution, 12 to 14 points) and three-card support. Opener has a five-card suit that he does not care to rebid, preferring to be passed out in responder's suit if partner has a minimum also.

Open one heart, and bid three diamonds over two diamonds, holding:

♠ x x   ♡ J x x x x   ◇ A Q x   ♣ A Q x

On rare occasions, opener may have five-card support to raise a minor suit response (he will never have a side *four*-card suit); but he will normally jump-raise if partner responds in opener's long suit:

♠ A K x x   ♡ K Q x x x   ◇ Q 10 x   ♣ x

Open one spade; if partner responds two hearts, jump to four hearts.

If opener jumps in a new suit over a constructive response, he has a very powerful two-suiter, plus 18 to 21 points, and slam is in view. Open one spade and jump to three hearts over a two-club or two-diamond response (or, for that matter, over the negative one-notrump step response) holding:

♠ A Q x x   ♡ A K J 10 x x   ◇ A x   ♣ x

AUCTION AFTER STRONG RESPONSES

Opener's rebids over the strong one-notrump response (one spade—one notrump is negative, remember) are the same as over a constructive suit response; however, the auction will proceed to game, for responder has a balanced 12- to 15-point hand. Opener shows his distribution and strength normally, and the proper contract can be reached without strain, since all bids are forcing.

OPENER	RESPONDER
♠ A Q x x x	♠ K x x
♡ A x	♡ K Q 10
◇ A J x x x	◇ Q x x
♣ x	♣ K J x x

OPENER	RESPONDER
1 diamond	1 notrump
2 spades	2 notrump
3 diamonds	3 spades
4 spades	Pass

Opener, with two equally long suits, starts with the lower-ranking. The one-notrump response is equivalent to a standard jump to two notrump, but it saves a round of bidding. Over the two-spade rebid, responder indicates good material in the unbid suits by bidding two notrump. Opener now shows that his diamond suit is a five-carder; responder shows spade support; and the best contract is reached after full investigation.

If responder jumps to two notrump over the opening bid, showing 16 to 18 points and balanced distribution, opener must rebid three notrump with any minimum hand, whether one-suiter or two-suiter, to sign off. When opener is in the stronger 15- to 17-point range, he makes the canapé rebid in his long suit, and slam investigation can proceed.

Responder's jump raise of opener's suit promises 10 to 14 points with five-card support, including two of the three top honors. This sets the trump suit if it is a major, even if opener has only three cards in the suit. Opener must sign off by raising to game with any minimum hand. Any new-suit rebid is an asking bid, looking for a slam.

OPENER	RESPONDER
♠ K x	♠ A x x
♡ Q J x	♡ A K x x x
◇ x x	◇ Q x x
♣ A Q x x x x	♣ x x

OPENER	RESPONDER
1 heart	3 hearts
4 hearts	Pass

Opener may not bid his club suit over the jump raise; this would initiate slam bidding, and he has a minimum. Four hearts must be a sound contract.

A jump shift by responder, except in the negative step suit, takes control of the hand and is an immediate asking bid. To jump to three clubs over a one-heart opening bid, responder might have some hand such as:

♠ —— ♡ K Q J x x ◇ A K x ♣ K Q x x x

WHEN THE OPPONENTS COMPETE

If the opening one-diamond, one-heart or one-spade bid is doubled, responder now has a choice of *three* negative responses. The first is the raise, which is unaffected by the double. The second and third are the negative step response and the pass. Responder chooses among them according to his holding in opener's suit and the negative step suit (if it *is* a suit; over one spade it is notrump). With three cards in opener's suit, responder passes the opponent's double. With less than three-card support for opener's suit, and a preference for the negative suit, responder bids. He always bids one notrump over one spade doubled if he has fewer than three spades. The auction now proceeds normally.

♠ J x x x x ♡ x x ◇ K x x ♣ x x x

With this hand, responder will pass if one diamond is doubled; he will bid one spade if one heart is doubled; and he will bid two spades if one spade is doubled.

When the interference is an overcall, not a double, the two negative responses are the pass and the raise.

With enough for a constructive response, responder may make his normal bid over the double. However, he should redouble with three cards in opener's suit. And he may trap pass, intending to bid later if the opponents do not bid a suit he can double for penalties.

After an overcall, responder can show strength by making his normal bid, or by doubling for penalties. With a balanced 12-point or better hand that has no stopper in the enemy suit, responder cue-bids. Opener can then bid notrump with a stopper, or take his normal action.

When opener's right-hand opponent doubles the negative step response, opener will make his normal rebid except in two cases: With a minimum one-suiter, he passes instead of rebidding his suit; with five cards or more in the negative suit, he redoubles instead of bidding one notrump.

If the opponent's action over the negative step response is an overcall, opener will pass any minimum hand, one-suiter or two-suiter. With 15 points or more, opener makes his normal rebid. A penalty double is also possible; it would normally mean that the opponent has bid opener's long strong suit, so responder should almost never take out.

After the double of a constructive response, opener may make his normal rebid or pass, according to whether or not his hand has strong defensive potential. A redouble shows five cards or more in partner's suit.

Should right-hand opponent overcall after a constructive response, opener may double (normally when his long suit has been bid) ; pass to see whether partner wants to double (when he would stand for the double) ; or make his normal rebid.

ON DEFENSE AGAINST ONE-DIAMOND, ONE-HEART AND ONE-SPADE OPENINGS

When your opponents are using the Roman Club System, you can use virtually your normal defensive methods against their one-diamond, one-heart and one-spade opening bids. However, there are three features of these auctions with which you must be prepared to deal: the opening bid in a short suit; opener's rebid in his long suit; and the artificial negative step response.

Opening bids are made in three-card suits and weak four-card suits often enough to warrant an alteration in your usual defensive style. Give up the cue-bid of opener's suit. Treat a two-diamond overcall of a one-diamond opening bid as a simple overcall in diamonds, and do the same for hearts and spades. Too often, otherwise, the opening bid will steal your suit, and the auction may be up too high for you to back in at your second turn. Incidentally, if the opponents land at a three-notrump contract after opener bids two suits, give a lot of consideration to leading opener's first suit—particularly if his second suit is clubs.

Just as against the Neapolitan System, use the double of opener's second suit as a takeout, not a penalty, double. On this auction, for example:

OPENER	YOU	RESPONDER	PARTNER
1 diamond	Pass	1 heart	Pass
1 spade	Double		

you should have the pattern for a takeout double of spades—length in hearts, diamonds, and clubs. A typical hand would be:

♠ x   ♡ A Q x x   ◇ A J x x   ♣ Q 10 x x

However, if the response is constructive, almost always stay out of the auction.

The double of the negative step response:

OPENER	PARTNER	RESPONDER	YOU
1 heart	Pass	1 spade	Double

should not have any special significance concerning the suit you double. It should be a normal takeout double of *opener's* suit. In the example auction, and in the related sequence in which the response to a one-diamond opening bid is one heart, you presumably have tolerance for a penalty pass from partner —after all, you normally have a reasonably good spade holding when you double one heart. But you are not making a penalty double (in the sense that you have an overcall in the negative suit). If you *have* an overcall in the negative suit, overcall.

Your overcalls should be about as usual. You may take a chance on a doubtful bid if there is a negative response on your right. But if opener doubles you, run for the hills. He has at least five trumps.

Last, it is a good idea to use preëmptive jump overcalls against the one-diamond—one-heart—one-spade openings. A simple overcall at the two level will rarely bother opener—he has a long suit in reserve and he will normally be willing to come in at that level. But if you can get the auction up to the three level in a hurry, you may freeze the opponents out of their suit. When you have a six- or seven-card suit and sit behind a negative response, there is less danger than usual in making a preëmptive bid. This is not so much because responder is weak—he may have 8 or 9 or even 10 points—but opener does not have four cards in your suit; the only four-card suit he is allowed to have is the one he opened. Of course, it is possible that he has five cards in your suit, and the carnage will then be pitiful; but if you have a long suit, that is highly unlikely. Opener will seldom be willing to double with only three trumps, for responder would have to assume that he is doubling with five. So take your life in your hands and jump; it will pay big dividends in the long run.

IV. Opening Bids of Two

In the Roman System, opening bids of two clubs, two diamonds, two hearts, two spades and two notrump are neither
preëmptive nor game-forcing. They are usually made with
hands that would be opened with a one-bid in standard systems,
but they have distributional patterns that make them unsuitable
for a one-bid in *this* system.

TWO-CLUB AND TWO-DIAMOND OPENINGS

Opening bids of two clubs and two diamonds show three-
suited hands: 4-4-4-1 or 5-4-4-0 distribution. These patterns
are not balanced, so they may not be opened one club or one
notrump; nor are they two-suiters or long one-suiters, so one-
diamond, one-heart and one-spade openings are ruled out.
Therefore all three-suited hands must be opened either two
clubs (11 to 16 high-card points) or two diamonds (17 or
more high-card points). It makes no difference which three
suits opener has. His *rebid* will show his specific holding.

These are two-club opening bids:

♠ K x x x   ♡ A Q 10 9 x   ◇ A J x x   ♣ ——

♠ x   ♡ A Q x x   ◇ J x x x   ♣ A K Q x

♠ J x x x   ♡ A Q x x   ◇ x   ♣ K Q x x

These are two-diamond opening bids:

♠ K 10 x x   ♡ A   ◇ A K x x   ♣ A K x x

♠ A K J x   ♡ A K Q x x   ◇ ——   ♣ J x x x

Responder's first duty is to assess the game possibilities of
the hand. Opposite a two-club opening bid, 12 to 14 points or
more will generally produce game at notrump on sheer power
(7 to 9 or more points opposite two diamonds); and a suit
game may well be made with many fewer points when responder has strong distributional support for *two* suits, one of
which *must,* of course, fit opener. In order to try for game,
responder uses the artificial forcing bid of two notrump. This
asks opener, "Which are your three suits?" Opener replies by
bidding three in his singleton or void, thereby guaranteeing
possession of all the other suits.

After opener replies to two notrump, when responder has
four cards or more in one of the unbid suits he can invite game

by bidding this suit under the game level (opener will pass with a minimum, raise with a maximum) or he can jump directly to game. And when responder's only suit has been bid by opener (indicating the suit opener does *not* have), responder signs off with three notrump. Exceptionally, responder —with a *very* long, strong holding in the suit opener has bid —may decide to pass and give opener the pleasure of being declarer with a singleton or void in trumps. Let us see how this works:

OPENER	RESPONDER
♠ Q x x x	♠ K 10 x x
♡ ——	♡ Q x x x x
◊ K Q x x x	◊ A 10 x
♣ A J x x	♣ x

OPENER	RESPONDER
2 clubs	2 notrump
3 hearts	4 spades
Pass	

After the two-club opening, responder is sure that he wants to play in game, for opener has at least four cards in one of the majors. The two-notrump response is answered by opener's rebid in his short suit. Now responder jumps to game; a three-spade bid would be merely invitational. As it happens, opener would accept the invitation with the hand he has; but with a singleton heart and only four diamonds, opener would pass three spades and a fine play for game would be missed.

OPENER	RESPONDER
♠ K Q 10 x	♠ x x x
♡ A K x x	♡ J 10 x x
◊ K Q x x	◊ J x x
♣ x	♣ K Q x

OPENER	RESPONDER
2 diamonds	2 notrump
3 clubs	3 hearts
Pass	

Responder tries for game, since he knows that opener is strong. Responder would not have bid two notrump over a two-*club* opening. However, opener's three-club reply tells responder that his K-Q-x club holding is of doubtful value.

Over a three-diamond or three-spade rebid, responder would have bid four hearts, but over three clubs, three hearts is enough. Opener has a bare minimum for his two-diamond opening and so passes. He would have gone on to game with a club void or with greater high-card strength.

OPENER	RESPONDER
♠ ——	♠ Q J x x x
♡ A J 10 x	♡ x x
◇ A K J x x	◇ Q x x
♣ A J 10 x	♣ K x x

OPENER	RESPONDER
2 diamonds	2 notrump
3 spades	3 notrump
Pass	

Responder has quite enough for two notrump over two diamonds. He would need another ace to bid it over two clubs. (If opener had a small heart instead of the ace, and responder had the ace in place of a small one, the auction would start two clubs—two notrump and proceed identically.) Responder would have been interested in a very high spade contract after any other reply, but over three spades he must take his chances in three notrump.

OPENER	RESPONDER
♠ K J x x	♠ x x
♡ Q 10 x x x	♡ x
◇ ——	◇ A Q J 9 x x x
♣ A Q x x	♣ K x x

OPENER	RESPONDER
2 clubs	2 notrump
3 diamonds	Pass

Responder has a strong notion from the start that opener is short in diamonds, but he tries two notrump, hopefully. When opener makes the expected reply, responder passes out this misfit hand in the best contract. (Had the opening bid been two diamonds, however, responder would have tried three notrump just on power.)

When responder holds a weak hand and has no game ambitions, he merely bids his best or cheapest suit over the two-club

or two-diamond opening. When this response strikes one of
the opener's suits, opener will pass, or will raise with a near-
maximum to invite game. (Occasionally, opener may even jump
to game with a maximum two-diamond bid.) And when responder signs off in opener's singleton or void, opener bids
the next-higher suit—asking responder for his second choice.
Here are a few examples of sequences after a sign-off.

OPENER	RESPONDER
♠ A Q x x	♠ K x x
♡ K 10 x x	♡ x x
◇ x	◇ Q x x x x
♣ A 10 x x	♣ K x x

OPENER	RESPONDER
2 clubs	2 diamonds
2 hearts	2 spades
Pass	

Responder is not interested in game opposite a two-club
opening (he would bid two notrump over two diamonds) and
he signs off in his suit. Opener bids the next-higher suit to
deny diamonds; and now responder goes to two spades, showing his preference among opener's three suits. Opener, of
course, will never raise responder's second "suit," for if responder has two genuine suits and any reasonably good hand,
he bids two notrump directly.

OPENER	RESPONDER
♠ K Q x x	♠ x x
♡ A K J x	♡ 10 x x x
◇ A Q x x	◇ x x
♣ x	♣ Q x x x x

OPENER	RESPONDER
2 diamonds	2 hearts
3 hearts	Pass

Note that responder signs off with two hearts, not with three
clubs. If opener does not have four hearts, he will bid two
spades—and then responder can bid the clubs. Even over the
sign-off, opener tries for game, since he needs very little from
partner. If all he needed were four hearts—for example, if
he were void in clubs and had a fifth heart—opener could
jump right to game. But responder declines the invitation,

though if you reversed his heart and club holdings he would
bid the game.

OPENER	RESPONDER
♠ A K x x	♠ Q x x x x
♡ Q J x x x	♡ x x
◇ K Q x x	◇ A x x
♣ ——	♣ Q x x

OPENER	RESPONDER
2 clubs	2 spades
3 spades	4 spades
Pass	

Responder cannot afford to bid two notrump over two clubs
(as he would over two diamonds) because he is not prepared
to rebid three notrump over a three-spade reply. But when
opener moves toward game despite the sign-off, responder is
delighted to go on.

OPENER	RESPONDER
♠ A	♠ x x x
♡ J 10 x x	♡ x x x
◇ A K Q x	◇ x x
♣ A K x x	♣ Q 10 x x x

OPENER	RESPONDER
2 diamonds	3 clubs
3 notrump	Pass

Here the Roman System reaches an excellent game contract
that is virtually unbiddable by any other method. Responder's
sign-off encourages opener to gamble on three notrump, for
he will have a fine play opposite any five clubs in partner's
hand.

When an opponent doubles the two-club or two-diamond
opening for takeout, responder guides himself according to
whether or not he was going to make the "positive" two-
notrump reply. If he was, he redoubles over the double with
at least three cards in the minor suit opened; with fewer he
bids two notrump and the auction proceeds normally. If
responder intended to sign off over the opening, he now passes
with four or more cards in opener's minor; otherwise he bids
his suit.

After an overcall, responder generally passes with the minimum hand. However, he may bid a suit (usually if he has *two* suits) to look for a part-score. With a hand worth a positive response, he should bid two notrump as usual, or, with strong trumps, he should double for penalties. Opener should take out the double only if he is void in the doubled suit.

When responder passes the overcall, opener should reopen the auction only if he has a maximum. Then he can double for penalties, or bid the next-higher suit, or bid his five-card suit if he is void in the opponent's suit. If each opponent has bid a suit, opener doubles if he is short in the first-bid suit and bids two notrump if he is short in the second.

If opener's right-hand opponent doubles the response, opener ignores the double and makes his normal bid. But if the opponent overcalls after a suit response, opener raises partner with a singleton in the enemy suit; he himself will double if he has both the opponent's and partner's suits (to give partner the choice of defending or playing the hand) ; and he will bid a new suit if he has a five-card suit and a void in the opponent's suit (and therefore support for partner).

Last, if the positive two-notrump response is overcalled, opener doubles with length in the suit bid, passes with a singleton in the suit, and bids his five-card suit when void in the opponent's suit.

TWO-HEART, TWO-SPADE
AND TWO-NOTRUMP OPENINGS

Hands that have a long diamond, heart or spade suit and also a shorter or equally long club suit cannot be opened with one-bids in the Roman System. If the opening bid is one heart, for example, and opener rebids in clubs, he unconditionally guarantees more clubs than hearts; in fact, he is as likely as not to hold only *three* hearts with five or six (or even seven) clubs. Therefore, the distributional patterns with four or five clubs plus a four-card or longer diamond, heart or spade suit are opened two hearts, two spades, or two notrump. The opening bid of two hearts shows at least five hearts and at least four clubs; two spades shows at least five spades and at least four clubs; two notrump shows at least five *diamonds* and at least four clubs. (Remember, standard two-notrump openings are opened one club in Roman style.) The following hands are opened with two-bids:

1. ♠ K x x   ♡ A Q 10 x x   ◇ x   ♣ K J x x
2. ♠ A K 10 x x x ♡ x   ◇ x   ♣ Q J x x x
3. ♠ K x   ♡ x   ◇ A K x x x   ♣ A K x x x

Hand 1 is opened two hearts; hand 2 is opened two spades; hand 3 is opened two notrump.

AFTER TWO HEARTS OR TWO SPADES

When the opening bid is two hearts or two spades, responder will normally take one of the following actions: pass; raise to three; jump to four; show a preference for clubs; take out in a new suit; bid two notrump. Let us examine each.

Two-heart and two-spade opening bids are not forcing; responder should usually pass with 0 to 6 points and with many 7-point hands. Responder is in very good position to evaluate the quality of his points and distribution: High cards in the major suit opened and in clubs are golden, while minor honors in the other suits must be devalued. Length in opener's major is the most valuable distributional asset, for the most likely game contract is in that suit, but great club length is desirable (opposite a two-spade opening, four spades to an honor and a singleton club might produce game out of thin air) while three small clubs may be a deadly holding. In general, then, responder weighs his values in support of opener's major suit, with particular attention to his club holding, and passes 0- to 7-point hands with poor support (and no great preference for play in clubs) but may act with 5- or 6-point hands that have excellent support.

Pass a two-heart opening bid with:

1. ♠ Q J x x x   ♡ x x x   ◇ Q x   ♣ J x x
2. ♠ K Q x x   ♡ x x   ◇ Q x x x   ♣ x x x

But respond with:

3. ♠ A x x x x   ♡ Q x x   ◇ x x x x   ♣ x
4. ♠ Q J x x x   ♡ x   ◇ x x x   ♣ J x x x

Hands 1 and 2 have their values in the wrong suits and are poor for play in hearts. But hand 3 has game possibilities, and hand 4 must play in clubs, not in hearts.

Responder's most common action is to raise opener's major, either to three as an invitation, or to game. The single raise promises three-card or longer support and has a wide range in points, going from a hand like example 3 above, with good distributional support, up to an 11- or even 12-point hand with flat distribution and poorly located honors:

♠ Q J x   ♡ Q J x   ◊ K Q J x   ♣ x x x

The average value of the single raise is 8 to 10 points. Opener will go on to game with 15 or 16 points, or more, and 5-4-2-2 distribution; he may bid again with as little as 11 or 12 points if he has freakish shape and strong suits.

The jump raise to four in opener's suit is a closing bid made with three-card or longer support. This response too has an elastic minimum, varying with the quality of the points and distribution; normally it is based on 11 or 12 points, or more. However, responder may jump to four, semi-preëmptively, with length in opener's suits and shortness in the unbid major. Here are some typical jumps to four spades over a two-spade opening bid:

♠ A Q x x   ♡ x x x   ◊ x x x x   ♣ K Q

♠ A x x   ♡ Q x x   ◊ A K x   ♣ x x x x

♠ K 10 x x   ♡ A Q x x x   ◊ x x x   ♣ x

♠ Q x x x x   ♡ x   ◊ x x   ♣ K J x x x

When responder has a distinct preference for clubs over opener's major, he can sign off by bidding three clubs. This is equivalent to passing the opening bid, and opener will not move towards game except with a freak hand. Usually, the three-club response indicates a singleton in the opening major.

If responder wishes to suggest *game* in clubs, he jumps to *four* clubs. This is nonforcing but invites opener to go to game if he has more than minimum values. This bid is used by responder when he knows that the hand *must* play in clubs.

Normally, however, responder will not wish to give up on a three-notrump possibility. He can find out a great deal more about opener's distribution by bidding two notrump.

The response of two notrump is used whenever delicate investigation is necessary to find the best contract. Two notrump over two hearts or two spades is artificial and forcing; it asks opener to specify his distribution.

Opener rebids three clubs to show 5-4-2-2 shape. With 5-4-3-1 or 5-5-3-0, opener bids his three-card suit (with 5-5-3-0, he will "rebid" clubs next, completing the picture).

With a six-card major, opener rebids it; if he has five clubs also, he will bid clubs next. With 5-5-2-1 distribution, opener answers three notrump.

Let us give responder an example hand and see how the auction develops:

♤ x x   ♡ A J x x x   ◊ K J x   ♧ A x x

This is responder's hand. The opening bid is two spades. Responder bids two notrump. Now, if opener rebids:

Three clubs, showing five spades, four clubs, and two doubletons, responder bids three notrump.

Three diamonds, showing five spades, four clubs, three diamonds, and a singleton heart, responder bids three notrump. If opener, instead, has five clubs and no hearts, he will bid four clubs over three notrump and responder will raise to five clubs.

Three hearts, showing five spades, four clubs, three hearts, and a singleton diamond, responder bids four hearts.

Three spades, showing a six-card suit, responder raises to four spades.

Three notrump, showing five spades and five clubs, responder bids four clubs. Opener can raise to five clubs, pass, or rebid a semisolid five-card spade suit.

Clearly, therefore, responder tends to bid two notrump over two hearts or two spades when his hand has game-going strength and any of these features: five cards in the unbid major (to discover if opener has three-card support) ; a doubleton in opener's major (to learn whether opener has a six-card suit) ; three or four clubs (to decide between three notrump and five clubs).

When does responder bid a suit of his own—diamonds or the unbid major—over the two-heart or two-spade opening? With only a five-card side suit, responder will prefer to check for three-card support by using the two-notrump response (although if opponent's action robs him of the two-notrump bid, responder will bid a five-card suit)—so the suit takeout is made in a suit that does not require three-card support. However, the suit takeout may also be designed to investigate slam possibilities; then it will be followed by a jump in opener's major or in clubs. The response in diamonds or in the unbid major is therefore forcing. (A *jump* response is an asking bid—see Slam Bidding.)

If an opponent enters the auction over the opening two-heart or two-spade bid, responder tends to ignore the interference and make his normal bid. However, a redouble after a takeout double indicates a strong defensive hand and the desire to penalize the opponents. And the double of an overcall is, of course, for penalties.

Bidding sequences that follow the opening bid of two notrump have many similarities to those inaugurated by two hearts or two spades. But the mood of the auction is different: Opening major-suit two-bids immediately suggest a likely game contract, whereas the two-notrump opening, announcing a two-suiter in the minors, has dimmer prospects; responder is eager to raise opener's *major* suit, but he can seldom generate much enthusiasm for an 11-trick diamond game. In fact, the two-notrump opening, although it is not a "weak" bid, has a preëmptive flavor, for opener has at least nine minor-suit cards and must be afraid of the opponents' majors. Occasionally, a 9- or 10-point hand may be opened two notrump for this preëmptive effect, particularly third hand, non-vulnerable.

However, game is by no means out of the question, for responder may be strong. Responder can raise to three notrump with good material in the majors and fitting cards in the minors —hands such as:

♠ Q J 9 x   ♡ A K x x   ◇ K x x   ♣ x x

♠ K Q x   ♡ Q J x   ◇ Q x   ♣ A 10 x x x

He can jump to four diamonds to invite opener to go on with a maximum or pass with a minimum. More often, though, he will probe for game by responding three clubs.

The three-club response is analogous to the two-notrump response over a two-heart or two-spade opening. Opening bidder specifies his distribution in reply: three diamonds means 5-4-2-2; three hearts means a three-card heart holding; three spades means three spades; three notrump means five or more diamonds and five clubs with no three-card major; four clubs means a six-card *diamond* suit.

Responder uses the three-club bid to find a 5-3 major-suit fit, to discover whether opener's distribution is suitable for notrump, or to check on the length of opener's club or diamond suit. Here is a typical sequence:

OPENER	RESPONDER
♠ K x x	♠ A x x x
♡ ——	♡ Q J x x x
◇ A Q x x x	◇ x
♣ A J 10 x x	♣ K Q x

OPENER	RESPONDER
2 notrump	3 clubs
3 spades	3 notrump
4 clubs	5 clubs
Pass	

Responder's conventional three-club bid is made primarily in the hope that opener has three hearts. When the reply shows three spades instead, responder retreats to three notrump. Now opener completes the picture of his distribution by "rebidding" his clubs, and responder raises to the sound game contract.

Responder's (forcing) takeout to three hearts or three spades over two notrump again shows either a long, strong suit that does not need three-card support, or interest in a slam, based on a good minor-suit fit. But in competition a five-card major suit may be bid.

To sign off with a weak hand, responder can pass if his hand is suitable for play in notrump. Or, he can jump to *four* clubs (with four-card support or better). Most often, he will sign off with three diamonds, running for safety into opener's long suit. This sequence (opener: two notrump; responder: three diamonds) occurs in a high percentage of the hands that start with a two-notrump opening. Here is an example from the 1957 World Championship:

East dealer
Both sides vulnerable

```
                        NORTH
                        ♠ 9 8 6 4 3 2
                        ♡ Q 10
                        ◇ 9 7 2
                        ♣ 9 2
          WEST                            EAST
          ♠ K J 10 7                      ♠ Q
          ♡ A K 8 5                       ♡ 9 7 6 3 2
          ◇ J 6                           ◇ K 10 3
          ♣ Q 10 5                        ♣ A J 6 3
                        SOUTH
                        ♠ A 5
                        ♡ J 4
                        ◇ A Q 8 5 4
                        ♣ K 8 7 4
```

EAST	SOUTH	WEST	NORTH
Pass	2 notrump	Pass	3 diamonds
Pass	Pass	Pass	

The American West was unwilling to enter the auction at the three level after partner had passed, so the Italians "stole" the hand. They were set three tricks but scored a handsome profit, for, when the hand was replayed, their teammates bid the East-West cards to four hearts (after a normal one-diamond opening bid by the American South) and made five.

Over enemy interference, responder makes his normal bids. However, he may double overcalls for penalties, or redouble after a double to suggest punitive action. If he passes over a takeout double, he prefers clubs to diamonds and asks opener to rescue himself into clubs.

ON DEFENSE AGAINST THE ROMAN TWO-BIDS

The foregoing example indicates the necessity for concerting a defense against these opening two-bids. Since opener usually has the strength of a normal one-bid, it is uncomfortable to enter the auction at the two or three level. But it is often more dangerous to stay out of the bidding than it is to come in, for the hand may belong to you. A different defense is necessary against each variety of two-bid.

AFTER TWO CLUBS OR TWO DIAMONDS

The basic rule for entering the auction after your Roman opponent opens two diamonds is "don't." Opener has a very strong hand, and there is an even chance that he holds your suit. It is hardly conceivable that you have a game and it is more than likely that you will take a whopping penalty. If you have it firmly in mind that you are *not* to bid, you will recognize the exceptional situations where you break the rule—eight-card suits, strong seven-card suits, and, above all, freakish two-suiters (with two long suits, you have an excellent chance to strike opener's singleton or void in one). But when in doubt, pass; and when not in doubt, doubt a little. Just about your only safe action is with a normal diamond overcall: Double for penalties.

The situation is quite different when the opening bid is two clubs. Now you know opener has a minimum in high cards and competition is not suicidal. But it is still dangerous, for your trump suit is not going to split favorably: Opener has four trumps, or else they are massed behind you in responder's hand. Still, you dare not stay out of the auction with strong hands, for you may well have a game.

When two clubs is opened on your right, you have four actions available: a simple overcall, a jump overcall, a two-notrump overcall, and a double. The nonjump overcall (two diamonds, two hearts, two spades, or three clubs) should always show a strong hand—at least an opening bid—with a five-card or longer suit. A suit of good quality is desirable but not imperative, for it is hard for the enemy to double you; opener's partner will be afraid of a skimpy opening bid with a singleton or void in your suit, and if he passes, opener will be reluctant to double for fear that his partner has very little strength. Both you and your partner should bear in mind that the contract you are pointing toward is three notrump. With as little as 24 points between the two hands, you will be a favorite to take nine tricks at notrump. The opponent who has most of the high cards has no long suit to run, and the whole distribution of the hand is marked for you by the opening bid. Avoid suit games unless you have such a good fit that you can afford a terrible split in trumps; play in three notrump whenever possible.

Jump overcall when you have a distributional hand light in high cards but with a long, strong suit. This is primarily a preëmptive device, intended to make it more difficult for the opponents to find their fit. Partner should usually pass your jump overcall; but he may put you in game with a wealth of top cards, and with a very good fit he may bid high as an additional preëmpt.

Overcall two notrump when you have a strong balanced hand, a normal 16- to 18-point one-notrump opening bid. This is far from safe, but notrump plays so well against a two-club opening bid that it is worth the risk. Partner should raise to three notrump with scattered values. He should *not* try to find a 4-4 major-suit fit, so any suit bid at the three-level, even three clubs, is a sign-off.

The double of two clubs should be used as a takeout bid, strictly for majors. To double, you should normally have five cards or more in each major; the very least you should have is 5-4. Remember that you are not particularly interested in finding a 4-4 fit, for you cannot get a good (3-2) break in the suit. With most balanced hands you should overcall, bid two notrump, or pass. If you double, your partner should bid a four-card major suit if he has one and he may answer in a three-card suit if he has a strong preference for one major as against the other. A two-diamond reply is artificial, asking you to pick your better major and denying a preference. Partner should jump to three or four in a major with four-card or longer support and fitting cards.

Pass the opponent's two-club opening with balanced hands of 15 points or less; also, pass all 4-4-4-1 hands. You may get a chance to enter the auction later.

When do you enter the auction at your second turn? Never, if the response has been two notrump, the opponent's game try. But if responder has signed off in a suit, you may well decide to take belated action. If the opponents have found a fit, on some auction such as:

OPENER	RESPONDER
2 clubs	2 hearts
Pass or 3 hearts	

you may back in with a takeout double, normally with 4-4-4-1 pattern and always with four-card support for the unbid major or majors. This is relatively safe action, for both opponents are limited and if they have a fit you probably have one too.

The belated double has an entirely different meaning when the opponents have *not* found a fit:

OPENER	RESPONDER
2 clubs	2 hearts
2 spades	

Here a double is for penalties; you have a balanced hand (presumably 12 to 15 points) with four cards in the bid suit. The enemy is up at the two or three level with minimum values and no fit, so there may be rich pickings. Incidentally, these reopening takeout and penalty doubles may also be used against sequences that start with two diamonds, but, of course, with much greater caution.

When you are in fourth position, and two clubs is opened on your left, your actions are simple: You have had the benefit of hearing the response. If responder bids two notrump, pass unless you have a freak. If responder signs off in a suit, use normal defensive bidding: a double is for takeout, with emphasis on unbid majors, and shows high-card strength; an overcall shows a strong suit and distributional values.

Your *reopening* doubles are the same as in the direct position. They are for takeout if the opponents have found a fit, for penalties if they have not.

Last, a word of advice about your opening lead: If the opponents reach a suit contract after an opening bid of two clubs or two diamonds, lead trumps. This is almost always the best defense against the three-suited pattern.

DEFENSE AFTER TWO-HEART AND TWO-SPADE OPENINGS

Defense against an opening bid of two hearts or two spades is much less complicated, since you know a great deal about opener's distribution. Bearing in mind that *any* action is dangerous and requires solid values, since you are entering the auction at a high level, you should:

Double, for takeout in diamonds, or particularly, in the unbid major;

Overcall, to show a strong suit and game ambitions;

Jump overcall, with a *very* strong suit as a preëmpt, and to suggest a sacrifice;

Bid two notrump, as a natural bid with a powerful balanced hand or, more likely, with a long, strong diamond suit and stoppers.

Any double you make after previously having passed is for penalties.

DEFENSE AFTER A TWO-NOTRUMP OPENING

The opening bid of two notrump gives you much greater problems, for the hand may very well "belong" to your side (since opener has only minor suits), yet it is never pleasant to plunge into the auction in the blind at the three level. However, the two-notrump opening presents you with opportunities also, for the opponents are up at the three level themselves and may be ripe for a penalty, so your defensive bidding must be geared to locating major-suit fits when you have good distribution and to preserving the possibilities for a penalty double when you have a balanced hand.

Your principal weapons are the penalty double and the cue-bid of three diamonds (which is for a takeout; opener must have at least five diamonds, remember). You should double with strong balanced hands—16 points or more—or with 13 points at least and excellent defense against the minor suits. Partner is encouraged to double any minor-suit takeout by responder, or to pass it around for *you* to double. The message that you give partner with your double of the two-notrump opening is, "The opponents have bitten off more than they can chew; let us collect a penalty."

You bid three diamonds for takeout over two notrump when you have at least four cards in each major suit. The minimum high-card content varies with your distribution: With 4-4 you would need a sound opening bid; with two strong five-card suits, 9 or 10 points might suffice; with a freak, you need very few high cards. Partner can sign off by bidding three hearts or three spades (if necessary, in a three-card suit) or, with about 10 points and good support, he can jump to game. If partner wants *you* to pick the suit, he cue-bids four diamonds.

When you have one strong major suit and not the other, you can overcall. Overcalls, because of the level at which they must be made, are not "nuisance" bids based on distributional values alone—they are game tries. The three-club overcall is natural (opener may have only four small clubs) but obviously must be used with caution.

Pass any hand that does not fall into one of the categories above, even a rather strong one such as:

$$\spadesuit K x \qquad \heartsuit K J x x x \qquad \diamondsuit A x x \qquad \clubsuit K x x$$

You are not quite powerful enough to double; your heart suit is too broken for an overcall; you may not bid three diamonds without spade support. True, you may miss a heart game or a part-score, but the opponents are entitled to get a good result now and again. Basic to effective defense against any high bid is the willingness to be "fixed" by it, otherwise you will take too many sets.

Pass also if you have excellent defense against diamonds but not against clubs; a hand such as:

$$\spadesuit A x x \qquad \heartsuit K Q x \qquad \diamondsuit A J 10 x x \qquad \clubsuit x x$$

You are strong enough to double the two-notrump opening, but if you do, responder can pass to show clubs. If you pass, he would have to bid *four* clubs to sign off, since three clubs is conventional. Wait to double at your next turn. Any delayed double is for penalties.

In fourth position, with two notrump opened on your left, you hear the response before you need act. If responder passes, double with good high-card content and cue-bid three diamonds with *any* unbalanced offensive distribution. The opponents may be in trouble, so tend to double with 4-4 in the majors. Either the double or the cue-bid may be shaded a bit.

If responder runs to three diamonds over two notrump, your double gives your partner the option: He can pass for penalties, or take out, or jump in a good major suit. When you have a distributional hand with both majors and cannot stand a penalty pass of your double, take your chances with a four-diamond cue-bid.

If responder jumps to four clubs over two notrump, again your double gives your partner the option of passing or bidding, but this time it has a strong penalty flavor. You can bid four diamonds for a major-suit takeout.

V. Slam Bidding

Slam bidding may, of course, follow any of the various types of opening bid in the Roman Club System. We have already examined in some detail the specialized sequences initiated by the two types of strong one-club opening, and occasionally by the one-notrump opening. All other slam bidding is handled through the use of three tools: asking bids (most commonly); Blackwood (with a new Roman wrinkle); and a five-notrump jump to check on trump quality.

Asking bids are used to locate specific controls. Whenever either partner is sure that the combined hands have the points for a slam and wants to make certain that the opponents cannot take the first trick in one particular suit, or whenever either player feels that a slam can be made if partner has a key feature—an ace, king, void, or singleton—in a particular suit, he ASKS.

After the trump suit has been established—either by direct support, or indirectly through those special step sequences in which partner shows both the quality of his support and the quantity of his points—any bid in a suit other than trumps is an asking bid. Also, immediate jump shifts by responder over opening bids of one diamond, one heart, and one spade (except in the negative suit); jump shifts over two-heart or two-spade openings (except in clubs); jump shifts over two notrump (except in clubs and diamonds); and jump shifts over two clubs and two diamonds—all are asking bids. The answers are given by steps. The next-higher bid—counting notrump—is one step; the bid above that is two steps, etc. Responder shows his controls in the asked suit as follows:

> 1 step = no control
> 2 steps = king or singleton
> 3 steps = ace or void
> 4 steps = A-K or A-Q

Let us see how this works.

OPENER	RESPONDER
♠ x x x	♠ Q x x
♡ A J x x	♡ K Q 10 x x
◊ A K Q x x	◊ x
♣ A	♣ K Q J x

OPENER	RESPONDER
1 heart	3 hearts
3 spades?	3 notrump
4 hearts	Pass

After the response, opener knows that partner has five hearts with the king and queen, and a strong hand. A slam contract will be a good bet if there is a spade control, so opener asks in spades. The one-step answer says no control, so opener signs off safely at the four level. Even five hearts is too high on this hand.

OPENER	RESPONDER
♠ K Q x	♠ A x
♡ K Q x x x	♡ A x
♢ x	♢ Q x x
♣ Q x x x	♣ A K 10 x x x

OPENER	RESPONDER
2 hearts	4 diamonds?
4 spades	6 clubs
Pass	

The two-heart opening guarantees four cards in clubs, so responder is understandably excited. Slam seems sure unless the opponents can cash two diamonds, so he asks in diamonds. The two-step answer announces second-round control, and the slam is bid.

OPENER	RESPONDER
♠ Q x x	♠ A K
♡ A x x	♡ K Q 10 x x x
♢ A K x	♢ Q J x x x
♣ Q 10 x x	♣ ——

OPENER	RESPONDER
1 club	2 hearts
3 diamonds	4 diamonds?
5 clubs	7 hearts
Pass	

Responder's jump to two hearts over one club is not an asking bid; it is a strong response guaranteeing five cards with two of the three top honors and 12 or more points. Opener now shows his fit and point quality—four steps shows a maximum in points and a top honor in hearts with at least three.

Responder now asks in diamonds, hearts being the agreed-upon suit. Opener's four-step reply shows ace and king (or ace and queen, but responder knows which). And all the key features for the grand slam are located.

After receiving the reply to an asking bid, the player who asks is boss. If he returns to the agreed-upon suit, partner must pass. However, the asker does not have to sign off or bid a slam—he may ask again in another suit or use Blackwood.

In the Roman System, any bid of four notrump is Blackwood, except for a few specific auctions treated earlier in this book. Obviously, Blackwood is used when either partner needs to know only the number of aces and kings partner holds. But the Roman responses even give an indication of which aces and kings partner holds. They are:

Five clubs = no aces or three aces.
Five diamonds = one ace or four aces.
Five hearts = two aces of the same color, or both major, or both minor.
Five spades = two aces different in color and rank.

So if partner answers five spades and you hold the ace of spades, he must have the heart and club aces. Diamonds and clubs are both minor suits; hearts and diamonds are both red suits. However, if he answers five hearts, all you can be sure of is that he does hold the ace of diamonds. He may have hearts and diamonds (red) or clubs and diamonds (minor).

After four notrump for aces, a bid of five notrump asks for kings and the responses are consistent with responses to four notrump, but at the six-level. But if four notrump has not first been bid, five notrump over partner's last bid of four notrump or higher asks for aces, not for kings. This usually occurs after a step response to an asking bid.

If you *jump* to five notrump (indicating that you could have bid four notrump for aces, but elected not to) you are asking partner about his honors in the agreed-upon trump suit. These are his responses:

Six clubs = none of the top three trump honors.
Six in the trump suit = one of the top three honors.
Seven in the trump suit = two of the top three honors.

If no suit has been supported directly or by steps, then opener's first suit is assumed to be the trump suit.

OPENER	RESPONDER
♠ A x x x	♠ Q J 10 x x
♥ K Q J x x	♥ A
◇ K x	◇ A Q J x x
♣ x x	♣ A K

OPENER	RESPONDER
1 spade	3 diamonds
3 spades	5 notrump
6 spades	Pass

Responder asks in diamonds by jumping over the opening bid. The two-step answer tells him that opener has second-round control. Now his only worry is the trump suit—opener probably has ace-king, but there is no need to gamble. The five-notrump convention is answered six spades—the trump suit, showing one of the top honors. One is not enough, so responder passes.

VI. Defensive Bidding

When the auction is started by an opponent's opening bid, Roman bidding is much closer to normal. Defensive bidding is not an integral part of the system (which has the artificial one-club opening as its core) and again it is reasonable to use your normal defensive tactics along with Roman offensive bidding. But in case you want to do as the Romans do, their defensive bidding, which has many distinctive features, is presented here.

These are your tools: Overcalls are normal, limited bids; the takeout double is stronger, but also limited; the one-no-trump overcall is a strong takeout double; jump overcalls and jumps to two notrump show two-suiters; the *jump* in the opponent's suit is a cue-bid, forcing to game.

Overcalls are much the same as in standard bidding. They have a wide range, going from very weak hands with long suits up to the strength of moderately good opening bids with distribution that is unsuitable for a takeout double (there is no strong *jump* overcall, remember). With no one vulnerable, these are all two-club overcalls after a one-heart opening bid:

♠ x x	♥ x x	◇ K x	♣ Q J 10 x x x x
♠ x x	♥ A x x	◇ x x x	♣ K Q J x x
♠ x	♥ x x x	◇ K x x	♣ A K Q J x x

As in Neapolitan style, very poor suits, even weak four-carders, may be bid at the one level, just to get into the auction.

Raises of overcalls are mildly invitational and semi-preemptive, and jump raises are strongly invitational but non-forcing. New-suit takeouts, however, are treated as forcing, except when made by a passed hand.

TAKEOUT DOUBLES

The takeout double normally has the range of 12 to 16 points.* When you double with the minimum point values, you tend to have support for all unbid suits; however, with maximum values, you may be doubling with a long suit of your own because you are too strong for an overcall.

Responses to the takeout double are unusual. When your partner doubles an opening one-bid in a suit and your right-hand opponent passes, redoubles, or bids one notrump, you respond in your *shortest* unbid suit. Partner then knows that you have support, or tolerance, for the other two suits, and bids his better holding. You can now pass, raise, or bid the third suit, according to the distribution and strength of your hand. Suppose the bidding goes:

OPPONENT	PARTNER	OPPONENT	YOU
1 club	Double	Redouble	?

You hold:

♠ J x x   ♡ x   ◇ A Q x x x   ♣ x x x x

Bid one heart! You are no longer forced to bid, because of the redouble, but you have enough for a free response. If partner rebids two diamonds, you will raise; if partner rebids one spade, you will *bid two diamonds* (be suspicious of partner's one-spade rebid after your short-suit heart response—he may have been trapped into bidding a three-card suit).

When your right-hand opponent bids a suit over partner's double (either a raise or a new suit), signals are off—your free suit-bids show length. However, a new action, the double, is available when a new suit is bid on your right:

OPPONENT	PARTNER	OPPONENT	YOU
1 club	Double	1 heart	Double

* You may occasionally double with more, for reasons of safety or bidding economy, but partner will play you for a 16-point maximum. However, if you *jump* in a suit after doubling, you show a *very* powerful one-suited hand, similar to a standard strong jump overcall.

This double is for takeout, showing a fair hand and a desire to play in one of the other two suits (spades and diamonds in the example auction). You might well have the same hand as the one with which you bid your singleton heart in the preceding example. And your rebids would be the same as in that example.

When partner has doubled one notrump, whether an opening or a response, you respond two clubs, artificially, with all weak hands. Any other bid shows positive value, 8 points or more and a genuine suit.

If you have a game-going hand after any of partner's takeout doubles, you can force with a jump in a long suit, or you may cue-bid the opponent's suit.

The one-notrump overcall starts at 17 points, where the double leaves off, and goes as high as 24 points. You should not have a wildly unbalanced hand, for partner is allowed to pass, but you do not need a stopper in the opponent's suit. These are all one notrump overcalls after a one-heart opening bid:

1. ♠ A K J x   ♡ x x   ◊ K Q J x   ♣ K 10 x
2. ♠ A J x   ♡ K x   ◊ A Q J x   ♣ A K J x
3. ♠ A x   ♡ K J x   ◊ A Q x x   ♣ Q J 10 x
4. ♠ A Q x x x   ♡ x x   ◊ A x   ♣ A K Q x

Partner will pass with 0 to 3 points. With 4 to 7 points he responds two clubs, an artificial denial. Over his two-club response, you rebid two diamonds to show a minimum (17 to 20 points), balanced hand; or two notrump with a maximum (21 to 24 points), balanced hand. You bid a suit to show a minimum unbalanced hand, and jump in a suit with the maximum. Partner now places the contract.

If partner has 8 points or more, he makes a positive response —any bid other than two clubs. The auction is game-forcing, and all bids are natural.

The jump overcall is a specialized preëmptive bid showing a specific two-suiter. The two suits are the one you jump in and the next *higher* ranking, not counting the opponent's suit. Thus a jump to two spades over a one-diamond opening bid shows spades and clubs; over a one-club opening bid, it would show spades and diamonds. Over a one-club opening bid, if you had hearts and diamonds you would jump to two diamonds; if you had spades and hearts, you would bid two hearts. Both suits are normally of five cards or more, but, exceptionally, you may have six of the suit you jump in with a secondary four-card suit. These are jump overcalls after an opening bid of one heart:

1. ♠ K Q 10 x x   ♡ x   ◇ x x   ♣ K J 10 x x
2. ♠ x   ♡ x   ◇ Q J x x x x   ♣ A J 10 x x
3. ♠ Q J x x   ♡ x   ◇ K Q J 10 x x   ♣ x x

With hand 1, bid two spades; with hand 2, three clubs; with hand 3, bid three diamonds. Note that these are not strong hands. Your objective is to disrupt the opponents' auction and to encourage partner to make a high preëmptive bid or to take a sacrifice in either suit.

With *powerful* two-suiters, you jump to two notrump over the opening bid. This is forcing and compels partner to bid three clubs (or three diamonds, if the opening bid was one club). If you now bid a suit, your two suits are the one you bid and the minor that partner has bid. If you have the two unbid suits, you rebid three notrump and force a preference from partner. These are jumps to two notrump if the opening bid is in one of your short suits:

♠ A K J x x x   ♡ x   ◇ K Q J x x   ♣ x
♠ x   ♡ K Q 10 9 x x   ◇ ——   ♣ A J 10 x x x

Remember that you may have to go to the four level before you get a preference from partner, so be sure that your suits and the vulnerability warrant this action. Here is an example auction, after your right-hand opponent opens one diamond:

YOU	PARTNER
♠ K Q J x x x	♠ x x x
♡ ——	♡ Q 10 x x x
◇ x x	◇ J 10 x x
♣ A Q J x x	♣ K x

YOU	PARTNER
2 notrump	3 clubs
3 spades	4 spades
Pass	

Partner's three-club response is forced, and your three-spade rebid shows a two-suiter in spades and clubs. Partner raises because he has a useful card, figuring you to have nine winners yourself, with his holdings solidifying your suits.

The strongest defensive bid is the jump cue-bid in the opponent's suit. (A nonjump overcall in the enemy suit is natural, promising length in the suit and nothing much else.) You should have 5-4-4-0 or 4-4-4-1 distribution with at least 20 or 21 high-card points. Bid three hearts over a one-heart opening bid with:

♠ A K J x   ♡ x   ◇ K Q J x   ♣ A Q J x

♠ K Q 10 x   ♡ ——   ◇ A K x x x   ♣ A K J x

Over opponents' preëmptive three-bids, four types of action are available. You can overcall, indicating a strong suit and minimum opening-bid strength. You can double with 14 to 18 points, with good support for at least two of the unbid suits. (Over your double, partner will make his cheapest genuine suit-bid with a minimum hand, jump to game in a strong suit, or cue-bid with a strong hand.) If you bid three notrump, you have either a long, running suit with a stopper in the enemy suit, or a powerful balanced hand, usually 19 to 23 points. Last, you can cue-bid the opponent's suit with overwhelming strength. (Partner will bid his best suit unless he has slam ambitions; then he will bid four notrump or, stronger yet, answer with a cue-bid of his own.)

AGAINST ROMAN DEFENSIVE BIDDING

When your opponents are using the Roman defensive bidding, it is well to be prepared for some of the special situations that arise. If they overcall, nothing unusual is happening, but be a little readier to double their skinny one-level bids than you are normally. Their takeout doubles are standard but the "shortest suit" response creates a new sequence. As opener, double the artificial response to indicate that you were going to rebid in that suit.

When your partner's opening bid is overcalled with one notrump, you should seldom feel like bidding, for your opponent is very strong. But if you have good support for partner, raise him; and if you have a six-card suit of your own, bid it. Any action you take should be based on distribution, not points, and is semi-preëmptive. Of course, with 9 points or more you can double one notrump, but if your partner is prone to open psychics, be suspicious.

The weak two-suited jump overcalls can be dangerous, for the partner of the overcaller is in excellent position to preëmpt to a high level if he has a fit in either suit. If you are responder, with 7 to 9 points and scattered values, you may be frozen out of the auction if you pass, but a free bid may excite opener unduly. Fortunately, there is a bid lying idle for you to use: the next-higher suit. This is the second suit of the overcaller, and you should never want to bid it naturally; you can bid it to tell partner, "I am not strong enough for a free bid, but I have some useful cards, so bid as high as you can afford to." If partner has opened one club, and your opponent jumps to two diamonds, bid two hearts with

♠ K J x x   ♡ K x   ♢ x x x x   ♣ J 10 x

This should virtually guarantee four spades, for this is the suit you are encouraging partner to bid. Should your left-hand opponent now jump to four hearts, opener, with:

♠ A Q x x   ♡ x x   ♢ A x   ♣ K Q x x x

can safely bid four spades. If you had passed over two diamonds, you would both be out of the auction.

Last, over the strong two-suited jump to two notrump, try to bid as responder if you have any shadow of excuse. The opponents are on their way to a high contract, and you may be able to push them up higher by bidding before they find their fit. Opener, also, should do his best to get the auction up to the four level in a hurry.

VII. Summary of the Roman Club System

Below is a résumé of the Roman System in outline form.

Open one club
1) With 4-3-3-3 or 4-4-3-2 distribution and 12 to 16 points.
2) With 4-3-3-3 or 4-4-3-2 distribution and 21 to 26 points.
3) With a standard forcing two-bid, particularly a two-suited hand.

Open one notrump
With 4-3-3-3 or 4-4-3-2 distribution and 17 to 20 points.

Open one diamond, heart or spade
With a one-suited or two-suited hand that has a five-card or longer suit.

Holding a one-suited hand, open in your long suit unless
1) you have 15 points or more and a suit too weak to be rebid with a jump; then open in a three-card suit (lower-ranking if possible, but not clubs) and bid your long suit next.
2) your long suit is clubs; then open in your lower ranking three-card suit and bid clubs next.

Holding a two-suited hand, open in the shorter suit, or in the lower-ranking (but not clubs) of equally long suits. However,

Open two hearts, spades or notrump
With a long heart, spade or diamond (with diamonds bid two notrump) suit and an equally long or shorter club suit (at least four).

Open two clubs or diamonds
With 4-4-4-1 or 5-4-4-0 distribution. Bid two clubs with 12 to 16 points. Bid two diamonds with 17 points or more.

Open three, four or five in any suit
With three of the four top honors in a very long suit that will provide enough winners to hold a set to 500 points.

When the opening bid was one club
The one-diamond response is negative, showing 0 to 7 points (may be slightly more if no major suit is held).

After a negative response

> Opener, with 12 to 16 points, bids a four-card major suit, or a three-card heart suit, or one notrump.
>
> Responder now bids the full strength of his hand.

The responses of one heart, one spade, two clubs and two diamonds are constructive, showing 8 points or more (9 points and a five-card suit for a minor-suit response).

After a constructive response

> Opener shows a maximum (15 or 16 points) by skipping over one notrump to bid a new suit, or by bidding two notrump over two clubs or diamonds.
>
> Opener shows a minimum by bidding one notrump, by bidding one spade over one heart, by bidding two in a suit over two clubs or diamonds, or by raising the response.
>
> Responder now signs off by passing a minimum rebid, by rebidding his suit, or by bidding a new suit lower in rank than his first.
>
> If responder reverses or jumps with his rebid, he forces to game.

The responses of one notrump, two notrump, two hearts and two spades are strong. One notrump shows 12 to 15 points balanced; two notrump shows 16 points or more, balanced; two hearts or spades shows 12 points or more, and a five-card or longer suit containing two of the three top honors.

OPENER'S REBIDS

Over a one-notrump response, opener bids two notrump with a maximum, a suit with a minimum.

Over a two-notrump response, opener shows his point-count by steps: two clubs with 12 or 13, two diamonds with 14, two hearts with 15, two spades with 16. (If responder next bids four clubs he is interested in slam, looking for a suit fit.)

Over a two-heart or two-club response, opener shows, by steps, whether he has a maximum or a minimum, with good or poor support. Responder places the contract.

The responses of three or four in a suit are preëmptive.

OPENER'S STRONG REBIDS

To show a balanced 21 to 26 point hand, opener *jumps* in notrump over the response. (With 25 or 26 points, he jumps to *three* notrump over one diamond.)

To show a standard forcing two-bid, opener jumps in a suit over the response (but bids only *two* clubs or *two* diamonds over a one-diamond response). Responder now indicates, by steps, his precise support for opener's suit.

When the opening bid was one notrump

Responder passes with a balanced 0 to 5 points.

Responder bids two clubs with 0 to 5 points to sign off in a suit. Opener must rebid two diamonds, and responder now passes with diamonds, or bids two hearts, two spades, or three clubs.

Responder suggests game by raising to two notrump with 6 or 7 points.

Three-heart and three-spade responses are invitational, promising a six-card suit containing 4 or 5 points with no outside strength.

The two-diamond response is "Stayman," asking opener to bid a four-card major suit.

Two-heart, two-spade, three-club and three-diamond responses are forcing to game. Opener rebids by steps to show maximum or minimum points, good or poor support.

Any game bid by responder is conclusive.

Responses of four clubs, four diamonds, four notrump and higher show responder's exact point-count.

When the opening bid was one diamond, one heart, or one spade

Responder may not pass. The single raise and the next higher bid are negative responses, showing 0 to 8 (or slightly more) points.

After the raise

Opener passes with a minimum; with 15 points or more he can try for game by bidding a new (long) suit or by re-raising.

After the negative step response

Opener signs off by rebidding his suit; invites by jumping in his suit.

If the negative response is in opener's long suit, he rebids one notrump with 12 to 14 points; "raises" the response with 15 to 17 points; jumps with 18 or more points.

With 18 or more points, opener jumps in a new long suit. Holding 12 to 17 points, he bids his new long suit at a minimum level. Responder may now pass, but should keep the bidding open with 8 points or more.

Opener jumps in notrump with 21 to 24 points and 5-3-3-2 distribution.

Any suit responses (other than the negative step) and the jump in the negative suit are constructive responses, promising 9 to 10 points or more.

After a constructive response

Game will be reached unless both partners have minimum values.

Opener shows a maximum by rebidding his suit. (A jump rebid is forcing.) Responder may pass, rebid his suit, bid two notrump, or bid a new (long) lower-ranking suit to sign off. Any jump or reverse is forcing.

Opener bids a new (long) suit with 12 to 17 points—with more he jumps in the new suit. Responder, with a minimum, raises, gives a preference, rebids his suit, bids a new long lower-ranking suit, or bids two notrump. Opener will now pass with 12 to 14 points, go on with more.

Opener rebids in notrump to show a 5-4-2-2 hand suitable for notrump play, containing an unbid five-card minor suit.

Opener may raise responder's two-level response with three-card support, but needs five cards to raise one spade to two spades.

Responses of one notrump and two notrump, the jump raise and jump shift, are strong. One notrump (except in response to one spade) shows a balanced 12 to 15 points. Two notrump shows 16 points or more. The jump raise promises five-card support containing two of the three top honors. The jump shift is a slam try, an asking bid.

OPENER'S REBIDS

Over one notrump, opener rebids just as over a constructive response.

Over two notrump, opener rebids three notrump with any 12- to 14-point hand, rebids in a suit with more.

Over the jump raise, opener signs off with a game bid, or asks for slam.

When the opening bid was two clubs or two diamonds

The two-notrump response is a game try. It shows 12 to 14 or more points over two clubs, 7 to 9 or more points over two diamonds (or else excellent distribution).

After two notrump

Opener rebids in his singleton or void suit. Responder may

now jump to game, invite with a suit-bid under game, or,
conceivably, pass.

A suit response is a sign-off. If opener fits the suit he will
pass or, with a maximum, raise. If he does not, he bids
the next-higher-ranking suit.

Responder now places the contract.

When the opening bid was two hearts
or two spades

Responder may pass with 0 to 6 points. A preference to
three clubs is discouraging.

Responder should raise opener's major with three-card or
longer support and 6 to 11 points, according to quality of
fit. He should jump to game with more points or with
excellent fit.

Responder may invite game in clubs by jumping to four
clubs.

The two-notrump response asks opener to clarify his distribution. Opener bids any three-card side suit, rebids a six-
card major, bids three notrump with 5-5-2-1 distribution,
bids three clubs with 5-4-2-2 distribution.

New-suit responses are forcing.

When the opening bid was two notrump

Responder may pass a weak hand suitable for notrump play.

Responder may sign off in diamonds with a bid of three
diamonds or in clubs with a bid of four clubs.

The three-club response asks opener about his distribution.
Opener bids any three-card major, bids three notrump
with 5-5 in the minors, bids three diamonds with 5-4-2-2,
bids four clubs with a six-card diamond suit.

Responder may invite with a jump to four diamonds, or
force with three hearts or three spades.

Slam bidding

After a trump suit has been established, new-suit bids are
asking bids. Responses are by steps, showing first- or
second-round controls in the asked suit.

Almost all four-notrump bids are Blackwood. Responses are:
five clubs for 0 or 3 aces; five diamonds for 1 or 4 aces;
five hearts and five spades for 2 aces. But five spades
shows that the aces are different both in color and in rank
of suit.

A *jump* to five notrump asks about honors in the trump suit.
Responses are: six clubs with none of the three top honors; six in the trump suit with one of the top honors; seven in the trump suit with two of the top honors.

Defensive bidding

Overcalls show hands of limited strength. Poor suits may be bid at the one level.

Takeout doubles show hands of 12 to 16 points (but followed by a jump are stronger).

If opener's partner does not bid a suit, doubler's partner responds in his *shortest* suit.

If opener's partner bids a new suit, doubler's partner may double to show length in the two unbid suits.

With a game-going hand, doubler's partner jumps or cue-bids.

The one-notrump overcall shows 17 to 24 points, not wildly unbalanced.

Partner passes with 0 to 3 points.

Two clubs is a negative response, showing 4 to 7 points. Any other bid is constructive, forcing to game.

The jump overcall shows a two-suited hand, in the suit bid and the next-higher-ranking unbid suit. It is a defensive, preëmptive measure.

The jump to two notrump shows a powerful two-suiter.

Partner must rebid three clubs (unless clubs were opened; then three diamonds). Opener bids three of a new suit to show that suit and partner's bid suit. Opener rebids three notrump to show the two unbid suits. Partner now places the contract.

The jump cue-bid is forcing to game, showing a powerful three-suiter. A simple overcall in opener's suit is natural and nonforcing.

THE STANDARD OR "NATURAL" ITALIAN SYSTEM

Just as the majority of bridge players in any country are unlikely to use complex systems such as the Neapolitan Club and Roman Club, the majority of Italian players use bidding methods that include few or no artificial bids. These players bid much like Americans who follow Goren and other authorities in what is called the "standard" American system. Nevertheless there are some characteristic differences.

Natural Italian bidding has been chiefly influenced by three systems:

1. The original Culbertson System, which the present Goren System greatly resembles. The usual bids and responses—that is, opening one-bids, responses and rebids made on fair hands—differ little from those in the Goren system of today.

2. The Acol System played by many of the best British players. In this system, the opening two-club bid is the only forcing opening bid and is artificial; but other two-bids are very strong, usually leading to games and often to slams. Raises are "limit bids," and a double raise is not forcing.

3. The "canapé" principle of the French authority Pierre Albarran. This has been discussed and illustrated in various other parts of this book. Briefly, it means that a player with a strong hand will first bid a short suit so that he can later show strength by reversing in his real suit, which is higher-ranking than the first suit. When a player does reverse, his second suit is at least as long as his first suit and probably is longer; and his hand is strong. For example:

OPENER	RESPONDER
♠ A x	♠ Q 10 9 x x x
♡ A K Q x x	♡ x x
◊ A Q x x	◊ J x x
♣ x x	♣ Q x

OPENER	RESPONDER
1 diamond	1 spade
2 hearts	Pass

155

With a weaker hand—for example, without the ace of spades—West would have made the normal opening bid of one heart. The diamond suit was bid first to permit the reverse bid in hearts, showing strength and guaranteeing a playable heart suit. However, the reverse bid is only strength-showing, it is not forcing, and East was within his rights to pass. He knew hearts would play at least as well as diamonds and perhaps better. The combined hands play well at hearts, and though they do provide some play for game at spades, four spades would not be a particularly favorable contract.

The natural Italian system was played in several European tournaments and in the 1957 and 1958 world-championship matches by the Italian pair of Massimo D'Alelio and Eugenio Chiaradia, though Chiaradia is the principal deviser of the Neapolitan Club system. In 1959, D'Alelio and Chiaradia shifted to the Neapolitan Club.

LIGHT OPENING BIDS

Opening bids are fairly normal, ranging from 12 to 14 points as in American systems, but on occasion quite a weak hand may be bid:

♠ A 9 6 3   ♡ Q 10 9   ◇ A 4 2   ♣ Q 10 8

First hand, with neither side vulnerable, D'Alelio made an opening bid of one spade on this hand. Most Americans would not open it; of those that would, the majority would bid one club.

ONE-NOTRUMP OPENING

There is just about as much unanimity (and just about as much variety) among Italian players as among Americans on the subject of opening notrump bids. Most Italians, like most Americans, prefer a fairly strong notrump bid, of 16 or 17 points; but some like weak notrumps (12 to 14 or 15 points), especially when not vulnerable. D'Alelio bid notrump on 5-3-3-2 distribution in the following case:

OPENER	RESPONDER
♠ A Q	♠ J 10 5 4
♡ K J 9	♡ A Q 2
◇ Q 10 5	◇ K J 6
♣ K Q 10 3 2	♣ J 6 5

OPENER	RESPONDER
1 notrump	2 clubs
2 diamonds	3 notrump
Pass	

Opener was D'Alelio; responder was Chiaradia. The two-club response was equivalent to the Stayman convention so widely used in the United States. It is a forcing response. It does not require a four-card major suit, though in this case Chiaradia had one. The two-diamond rebid was the usual denial of a four-card major. In all, the bidding was just as it might have been among American players. Opener easily made four notrump.

INTERMEDIATE TWO-BID

The opening bid of two clubs (artificial and forcing) is made on a balanced hand of 23 or more points; or with a very strong one-suited or three-suited hand. An opening bid of two in diamonds, hearts, or spades usually shows a strong two-suiter; but occasionally this intermediate two-bid may be made on a one-suited hand that is very powerful in playing strength but not quite strong enough in top cards for a two-club bid. For example:

OPENER	RESPONDER
♠ A K Q 10 9 5 4 2	♠ 3
♡ ——————	♡ A 9 8 7 3
◊ K 9 4	◊ Q 3
♣ 8 4	♣ A J 10 9 2

OPENER	RESPONDER
2 spades	3 hearts
3 spades	4 clubs
4 spades	Pass

East's three-heart bid was a positive response, showing strength. The negative or weak response to any two-bid is the next-higher suit: Two diamonds to two clubs, two hearts to two diamonds, etc. With a bust, responder would have responded two notrump.

NONFORCING JUMP RAISES

A double raise of a major suit shows strong support, but it is not forcing and the opener, with a minimum, may pass.

The double raise is slightly weaker than it is bid in America, by perhaps half a trick or 3 points.

OPENER	RESPONDER
♠ K Q 7 6 2	♠ J 9 8 5
♡ ———	♡ K Q 10 9
◇ Q J 9 3	◇ A 10 6
♣ K 6 5 3	♣ 9 4

OPENER	RESPONDER
1 spade	3 spades
Pass	

Despite the duplication of values in the heart suit, there happens to be a good play for game in the combined hands; and perhaps opener, with his five-card suit and good distribution to compensate for his shaded high-card strength, should have gone on. But with many other types of minimum or borderline opening bids, such as the one-spade bid shown above, opener would properly pass and avoid a dangerously high contract.

OTHER JUMP BIDS

As among most American players (though not the majority of America's international players) a jump overcall shows strength but is not forcing. Over an opening bid of one club on one's right, the following hand is a jump overcall of two hearts:

♠ 10 x   ♡ A K Q x x x x   ◇ A Q   ♣ x x

However, over an opponent's takeout double a jump response shows weakness and is preëmptive:

♠ x x   ♡ J x x   ◇ Q x   ♣ Q J 10 x x x

Partner opens one spade and right-hand opponent doubles. This hand justifies a jump response of three clubs.

DEFENSE AGAINST NATURAL
ITALIAN BIDDING

Defensive tactics against natural Italian bidding differ almost not at all from defensive tactics against any system that an American player might encounter a casual duplicate game or in a rubber-bridge game in a club or at home. The very few special defenses are required by the cases in which Italian bidding differs materially from American bidding.

When a double raise of an opening major-suit bid is passed by the opener in the usual American systems, fourth hand justifiably suspects a psychic opening bid and may strain a point to reopen. This approach would be suicidal when the double raise is not forcing, for the opener probably has a genuine bid, even though it may be a minimum.

Defensive tactics against canapé bidding are discussed in earlier sections, for canapé bidding is used even more in the Neapolitan and Roman Club systems than in natural Italian bidding. Since the canapé approach may be expected only on quite strong hands, which occur infrequently, it is a mistake to assume that the suit first bid is short, even when it is a minor suit.

Natural Italian bidding is as indefinite as American bidding in fixing the strength of the opening hand—with the one slight exception made by the intermediate two-bid, which slightly limits the strength shown by a one-bid—and overcalls and takeout doubles should be made normally, as they would be in an American game.

Other SIGNET KEY Books You'll Enjoy

HOYLE'S RULES OF GAMES (revised)
by *Albert H. Morehead* and *Geoffrey Mott-Smith*

Authoritative rules and instructions for playing hundreds of indoor games. New bridge bidding and scoring rules.
(#KD363—50¢)

HERE'S HOW by *Lawrence G. Blochman*

A brand new bar guide, prepared with the cooperation of the Overseas Press Club, for a thousand drinks.
(#Ks350—35¢)

ELECTRONICS FOR EVERYONE (revised and expanded) by *Monroe Upton*

This easy-to-read, authoritative book helps you understand today's wonders in the field of electricity.
(#KD351—50¢)

HOBBIES FOR PLEASURE AND PROFIT
by *Horace Coon*

A comprehensive, illustrated guide, with hundreds of intriguing suggestions for getting more out of leisure time.
(#Ks318—35¢)

THE HOUSEHOLDER'S MANUAL by *Richard Kent*

All aspects of home building, remodeling and repairing, with detailed information on financing. (#K312—25¢)

THE HANDY BOOK OF GARDENING
by *Albert E. Wilkinson* and *Victor A. Tiedjens*

How to grow flowers, vegetables, fruits and house plants, and do landscaping. (#Ks323—35¢)

HOW TO KNOW AMERICAN ANTIQUES
by *Alice Winchester*

How to recognize antiques such as silver, furniture, pewter, china and needlework. 300 drawings.
(#KD328—50¢)